1,001
BASEBALL
QUESTIONS
YOUR FRIENDS
CAN'T ANSWER

Dom Forker

A SIGNET BOOK

SIGNET
Published by the Penguin Group
Penguin Books USA Inc., 375 Hudson Street,
New York, New York 10014, U.S.A.
Penguin Books Ltd, 27 Wrights Lane,
London W8 5TZ, England
Penguin Books Australia Ltd, Ringwood,
Victoria, Australia
Penguin Books Canada Ltd, 10 Alcorn Avenue,
Toronto, Ontario, Canada M4V 3B2
Penguin Books (N.Z.) Ltd, 182–190 Wairau Road,
Auckland 10, New Zealand

Penguin Books Ltd, Registered Offices:
Harmondsworth, Middlesex, England

First published by Signet, an imprint of Dutton Signet,
a division of Penguin Books USA Inc.

First Printing, March, 1997
10 9 8 7 6 5 4 3 2 1

 REGISTERED TRADEMARK—MARCA REGISTRADA

Printed in the United States of America

Introduction

Baseball, like life, is usually a nine-inning game. Like life, the "National Pastime" is full of paradox and irony. The questions and answers in this book often bear this point out.

For example, Lou Gehrig of the 1925 Yankees broke into the starting lineup and went on to set a record by playing in 2,130 consecutive games. The record that he broke—1,307 consecutive contests—belonged to a 1925 teammate, Everett Scott.

In 1927, Babe Ruth hit his then-record sixtieth home run off Tom Zachary of the Senators. Two years later, Zachary won all 12 of his decisions for Ruth's Yankees. This record still stands as the most wins without a loss by a pitcher in a season.

The Yankees had three premier center fielders over a 44-year period—Earle Combs, Joe DiMaggio, and Mickey Mantle. They all ended up in the Hall of Fame. Combs and DiMaggio retired with identical .325 batting averages.

People flocked to Navin Field in Detroit on the last day of the 1938 season to see if Hank Greenberg of the Tigers, who had 58 home runs, could break Babe

Ruth's record of 60 home runs in a season. But after the doubleheader, they left the ballpark talking about Bob Feller, a 19-year-old pitcher, who struck out a record 18 batters in the first game, and *lost*!

Greenberg and Feller have another "trivia thing" in common. Hank won home run titles in 1940 and 1946, his last full season before World War II and his first full campaign after it. Feller led the league in both wins and strikeouts in his last full season before the war and his first full year after it.

"Hammerin' Hank," as I said, led the American League in home runs in 1946. After the season he was sold to Pittsburgh, where he tutored rookie Ralph Kiner, who won a record seven consecutive home run crowns during his first seven years in the majors.

In a similar scenario, Joe Page of the Yankees, who paced American League relievers in both wins and saves in 1947 and 1949, also moved on to Pittsburgh and in 1954 taught the forkball to Roy Face, who proceeded to save 193 regular-season games, as well as a record three games in the 1960 World Series.

Other examples include Johnny Vander Meer, who hurled a record two consecutive no-hitters for the 1938 Reds. In 1947, he looked on as teammate Ewell Blackwell came within two outs of equaling his feat.

And Nellie Fox, who was almost impossible to strike out with the White Sox. He was eventually moved to the Astros, where he trained Joe Morgan, a young second baseman, to be pitch-selective. Morgan went on to walk 1,799 times, setting a National League record.

The examples are endless. The phenomenon of teaching one's young is always going on in baseball, as in life. Mention almost any major-league player, and you think of his connection with another.

But baseball comparisons often lead to baseball disputes. I grew up in Bayonne, New Jersey, where major-league allegiances were divided equally between the Brooklyn Dodgers, the New York Giants, and the New York Yankees. We would argue baseball all day long—and all night long, too.

"Who's the best first baseman in New York—Gil Hodges, Monte Irvin, or Johnny Mize?" Division.

But this question, and any other like it, reinforces my point that you can take almost any comparison-and-contrast question and convert the subjects into tantalizing trivia topics.

When I think of Gil Hodges, I connect with a baseball player who hit four home runs in one game in 1950; a player who went hitless in 21 at bats in the 1952 World Series but rebounded to bat .364 in the 1953 Fall Classic; a player who drove home 100 or more runs for seven consecutive seasons, from 1949 to 1955; a manager who led the underdog Mets to a five-game victory over the surprised Orioles in the 1969 World Series.

Monte Irvin calls to mind a player who had to wait too long to get to the major leagues; a player who was one of the last base runners in World Series play to steal home without the aid of a double steal; an all-round player who batted .458 in that same 1951 World Series; and the same proud player that Dusty

Rhodes pinch-hit for *three* times in the 1954 Fall Classic.

Johnny Mize stirs up memories of a slugger who won four home run crowns in the National League, two with the Cardinals and two with the Giants; a slugger who tied for the home run crown in back-to-back years with the same player, Ralph Kiner; a slugger who has been the only left-handed batter in National League history to hit 50 (51) home runs in a season; a slugger who has been the only player to hit 50 home runs in a season while striking out fewer than 50 (42) times; a slugger who bowed out of the majors by leading the American League in pinch hits for three straight years; a slugger who became the only player in baseball history to bow out of the big leagues by performing on five consecutive world championship clubs.

But let's get back to those baseball comparisons of my youth.

"Who's the best second baseman in New York— Jackie Robinson, Eddie Stanky, or Billy Martin?" Dynamite.

"Who's the best shortstop in New York—Pee Wee Reese, Alvin Dark, or Phil Rizzuto?" Detonation.

"Who's the best third baseman in New York—Billy Cox, Bobby Thomson, or Gil McDougald?" Destruction.

"Who's the best catcher in New York—Roy Campanella, Walker Cooper, or Yogi Berra?" Demolition.

"Who's' the best center fielder in New York—Duke Snider, Willie Mays, or Mickey Mantle?" Devastation.

"Who's the best announcer in New York—Red Barber, Russ Hodges, or Mel Allen?" Depletion.

"Who's the best manager in New York—Charlie Dressen, Leo Durocher, or Casey Stengel?" Diffusion.

"Who's the best team in New York—the Dodgers, the Giants, or the Yankees?" Detention.

You get the idea. These comparisons would provoke almost any Dodgers, Giants, or Yankees fan from that era to argue from morning till night. I know who my choices are. Your picks could be different. But that's why we love this game of baseball. Former baseball pitching star Johnny Sain of the Boston Braves and the Yankees once told me, "Whenever you go to a baseball park, you always know that you're sitting next to an expert."

Is it still the same today? Do you still, during those alluring summer afternoons and restless summer evenings, argue baseball constantly? Can you still transcend the owners' and players' repeated attempts to "shoot themselves in the foot"? I hope so.

Jacques Barzun, the famous philosopher from Columbia University, once said, "If anyone wants to know the mind and heart of America, he had better study baseball."

But *1,001 Baseball Questions Your Friends Can't Answer* separates the baseball men from the baseball boys. Everyone may think he's a baseball expert. But in the final analysis, one comes to the conclusion that only a very few fans are baseball aficionados. This book gives you the opportunity to join that select group. Either you know the answers to the questions or you don't. One thing is definite, though: you'll enjoy one-upmanship on your friends after you read *1,001 Baseball Questions Your Friends Can't Answer*.

Let's start out with three bonus questions from the Dodgers, Giants, and Yankees of my youth.

1. Who was the Dodgers pitcher who hurled a no-hitter in his first month back from World War II (April 23, 1946)? (He won just two more games in the final year of his career.)

2. Who was the winning pitcher on the day Bobby Thomson hit the pennant-winning home run against Ralph Branca of the 1951 Dodgers? (Sal Maglie started the game.)

3. Name the Yankees pitcher who was the only hurler to throw a one-hitter in a World Series game—and *lose*! (He never started another major-league game.)

—Dom Forker
May 15, 1996

The Ground Rules

This book has 10 chapters and a total of 1,001 questions. We're going to round the questions off to 1,000 for scoring purposes.

After each chapter there is space for you to compute that section's season batting average. The average of the scores for all 10 chapters (seasons) represents your career batting average.

Keep in mind that 10 is a symbolic number. It could represent anything from a 5-year career to a 25-year career.

In the chapter on modern-day players, we simply ask the questions. We don't follow up with a clue statement. In all of the questions dealing with past players, however, we do give a follow-up clue statement. We want you to study your pitches before you swing at them.

Baseball interludes appear at the end of each chapter. In all, there are thirty of them. They represent your career World Series at-bats.

When you've finished this book, divide your total number of correct answers by 1,000, and you've got your career batting average. Then divide your total number of correct answers in the bonus questions by thirty, and you've got your career World Series batting mark.

Then turn to "Your Career Batting Average" and "Your Career World Series Batting Average" at the end of the book and see whose actual lifetime batting average (season and World Series) matches up with yours.

Good luck!

Chapter One

Willie, Mickey, and the Duke

1. Who has been the only player to lead each league in triples and homers? (In his last seven full seasons, 1909 to 1915, during the dead-ball era, he averaged 106 RBIs per season.)
2. Who was the player who got 1,815 of his 3,630 hits on the road and 1,815 of them at home? (A model of consistency, he led his league in triples five times and in runs five times.)
3. Who was the pitcher who amassed 363 career wins and 363 career hits? (He had 63 shutouts, the second highest number by a left-hander.)
4. What 1949 Philly had only three hits, all of which were home runs? (In seven games he had seven RBIs.)
5. What pitcher won the seventh game of the 1924

World Series and lost the seventh game of the 1925 Fall Classic? (He was 1–2 in the 1924 Classic and 2–1 in the 1925 Series.)

6. Who was the four-time home run champ who had a .609 regular-season slugging average and a .609 World Series slugging mark? (He won the batting title, the home run race, the RBI crown, and the MVP award with two different teams.)

7. Who was the 1966 Red who didn't enter one particular game until the eighth inning, yet hit three home runs in that contest? (He batted .538 for the 1969 Mets in the National League Championship Series.)

8. Name the pitcher who batted .211 in 11 seasons and .211 in five World Series. (In four seasons with the White Sox, he was 50–49; in five Fall Classics with the Yankees, he was 4–1.)

9. Edgar Martinez of the 1995 Mariners became the first right-handed batter in the American League to win two batting titles since what player of the 1930s and 1940s—who, by the way, was the only player from his team ever to win a batting crown?

10. In his second year in the majors, he led his league in batting (.380), hits (237), triples (17), and RBIs (131), a club mark that still stands. (Ironically, he hit only nine home runs.) Who was this 1927 flyhawk?

11. Who was the only catcher to win two batting crowns? (He was a .306 lifetime hitter.)

12. Who set the single-season batting high with

three different clubs? (He won seven batting titles.)

13. Name the Yankees infielder who got only two hits, both of which were home runs, in a losing World Series effort. (In the following World Series, he batted .417 and hit one homer.)

14. Who was the Hall of Famer who broke into the majors on a World Series loser and then, 22 years later, bowed out of the big leagues on a Fall Classic loser? (In between, this four-time home run champ played for two other World Series clubs, one a winner and one a loser.)

15. Who was the only player to hit four home runs twice in a World Series? (He hit 407 lifetime four-base blasts.)

16. In one decade the Red Sox had two players who won five batting titles with averages that did not exceed .326. One of them did it with marks of .326 and .320. Who was that .291 lifetime hitter?

17. The other one won three crowns, one with a .301 average, the lowest ever to lead either league. Name the .285 lifetime hitter.

18. Name the player who won two home run titles, 11 years apart. (He also won two batting crowns, in back-to-back years.)

19. Who drove home only 26 runs in a full season, but in that year's World Series delivered a record 12 runs? (He batted .252 during the season and .367 in the Fall Classic.)

20. Name the .322 lifetime hitter who ended his career

with 2,987 hits. (In his last season, with the 1934 Indians, he batted .293 and collected 98 hits.)

21. Who is the present-day pitcher who has had .500 seasons of 14–14, 15–15, and 16–16? (He has pitched in World Series in each league.)

22. Who won Rookie of the Year at age 19 and the Cy Young Award at 20? (He also struck out a rookie-record 276 batters.)

23. Who was the 1990 player whom the Reds intentionally walked a record five times in one game? Twice, he hit two home runs in one inning.)

24. What 1987 and 1988 player became the first infielder to hit 30 home runs and steal 30 bases in the same season—twice? (In 1991 he performed the feat a third time, but not strictly as an infielder.)

25. Name the Red Sox player who had career highs of 30 home runs and 100 RBIs one year and career lows of .171 and no homers the following season. (He suffered from vertigo.)

26. Who was the only player to bat .500 three times in the World Series? (He was a pitcher.)

27. Who became the first player to win a batting title while finishing the season in the other league? (He won two batting titles, five years apart.)

28. In 1985 he started 37 games, but didn't finish one of them. (Two years later, as a reliever, he finished 40 games and won the Cy Young Award.) Who is he?

29. Who won the Cy Young Award and Rookie of the Year in the same season? (In postseason play he was 4–1.)

30. Who was the only player to win Rookie of the Year and Most Valuable Player in the same season? (He won the batting title in 1979.)

31. Who is the pitcher who made the All-Star Team as a starter in 1988 and as a reliever in 1989? (He posted a league-high 38 saves in 1989.)

32. Who hit a single-season record six grand slams in one season? (He never hit one before or after that year.)

33. Who became the first player to hit three home runs on opening day? (The year before, he hit 47 home runs and drove home a league-leading 134 runs.)

34. Who became the first pitcher since Jim Palmer of the 1975–78 Orioles to win 20 or more games for four consecutive seasons? (He did it from 1987 to 1990.)

35. Who got 200 hits and 100 walks in a record four consecutive seasons? (He hit .300 in each of his first 10 seasons.)

36. Who became the first American League pitcher to win as many as 27 games since Denny McLain of Detroit won 31 in 1968? (He had a couple of dramatic confrontations with Reggie Jackson in the 1978 World Series.)

37. Who became the first player in history to hit 30 or more home runs in each of his first four seasons? (He hit a rookie-record 49 in 1987.)

38. Name the 1982–86 outfielder who became the first player since Willie Mays of the 1959–66 San Francisco Giants to drive home 100 or more

runs in five consecutive years. (He retired with more than 3,000 hits.)

39. Who was the most recent 200-game career winner to reach that plateau without the benefit of a 20-win year? (His highest win total was 18, with the 1987 Rangers.)

40. Who got a career-record 3,215 singles? (He batted .303 lifetime.)

41. Who was the only player to collect 250 hits while performing for a last-place club? (He won three consecutive home run crowns with the Phillies.)

42. Whose 21 triples set a single-season record for a switch-hitter in this century? (He won four other triple titles also, three of them with 15 triples.)

43. Who led his league in home runs for a record seven consecutive years? (They were his first seven years in the majors.)

44. Name the six-time home run champ who won a four-base crown with only 212 official plate appearances. (Two times he won three consecutive home run crowns.)

45. Only one catcher has won a home run crown. (He won two.) Who is he?

46. Name the only home run champ to be traded for the batting crown winner. (He once hit four consecutive home runs in one game.)

47. Who was the first Yankee to win back-to-back home run crowns. (He also won a triple title.)

48. Name the four-time home run champ who won a four-base crown the year before he left for

World War II and the season after he returned from it. (He also won four RBI titles, one with 183, the most by any right-handed hitter in the history of the American League.)

49. Who was the only player to win home run crowns with three different teams and hit more than 100 home runs with three different clubs? (He posted the highest career slugging average, .755, in World Series history.)

50. Who at 38 became the oldest player to win a home run crown? It was his only one. (He had 40-home-run seasons in each league.)

51. Who was the only player to hit more than 50 home runs and strike out fewer than 50 times in the same season? (They called him the Big Cat.)

52. Who became both the youngest and the oldest player to hit 50 home runs in a season? (He won four home run crowns and three triple titles.)

53. Who was the only player to hit his last three home runs in one game? (He did it with a team in the same city for which he first played, but in the opposite league.)

54. Who batted .408 in his first full season but didn't win the batting crown? (In his last year he hit .382, the highest for a final season, but didn't win the batting crown.)

55. Who batted .402 over a five-year period of time? (He won six consecutive batting crowns.)

56. Who was the American League player who batted .333 lifetime and collected 3,311 hits, but didn't win any batting titles? (He won four sto-

len base titles, the last two at the ages of 36 and 37.)

57. Who was the only player to hit for the cycle in both leagues? (He has also been a general manager in both leagues.)

58. Who seven times drove home 100 runs without hitting 10 home runs in those seasons? (Eight times he led his league in doubles, and eight times he led his league in batting, both records for the senior circuit.)

59. Whose 213 hits in 1986 are the most ever by a shortstop in one season? (His fielding average is also contending for the top spot in history.)

60. Who is the National League player who won the batting title with the lowest average in senior circuit history? (He also won it with the highest average, .394, since Bill Terry of the 1930 New York Giants hit .401.)

61. Who was the Hall of Famer who batted a single-season-high .433 for pitchers? (It was in his nineteenth year. He had never hit .300 before. But he did hit .348 in his final season, two years later.)

62. Name the two-time batting champ who has been the only right-handed swinger to hit .300 in each of his first 11 seasons. (In 1925 and 1927 he batted .384 and .392 respectively, but didn't win the hitting title either year.)

63. Who was the most recent player to win the batting crown without hitting a home run? (Clarence Beaumont of the 1902 Pirates and Zack Wheat of the 1918 Brooklyn Dodgers did it, too.)

64. Who was the oldest player (35) to win his first

batting crown? He did it in 1982. (A .303 lifetime hitter, he batted .300 with four different teams.)

65. Who, in his last nine seasons, averaged .363 but didn't win a batting title? (At another point in his career, he won a record nine consecutive hitting crowns.)

66. Who were the only brothers to finish one-two in a batting race? (Each of them led his league in hits. The runner-up did it twice.)

67. Who was the last playing manager to win a batting title? (Four years later, he won MVP honors.)

68. Who won a batting title when he hit .361 in his first full season and then never topped .300 again? (He never won a home run crown, but he hit 377 career circuit clouts.)

69. Who never hit 50 home runs in a season but hit 49 twice? (He hit 40 home runs in a season eight times.)

70. Only one Triple Crown winner did not drive home 100 runs in that triple-threat season. (He was a third baseman.) Who was he?

71. Two players who came up to the majors in 1951 turned in career slugging percentages of .557. (They both won four home run crowns, and each of them twice hit 50 home runs in a season.) Who was the National Leaguer?

72. Who was the American Leaguer?

73. Who posted the highest slugging average (.590) during the dead-ball era? (Only once, in 1920, his last season, did he end up in double digits (12) with home runs.)

74. Name the 1945 Yankee whose slugging average of .476 was the lowest by a league leader since 1919. (He won the batting title that year.)

75. Who was the last Yankee to record 400 total bases in a season? (He did it in 1937.)

76. Which one of the following players never recorded 200 hits in a season: Joe DiMaggio, Ted Williams, Stan Musial, or Rogers Hornsby?

77. Name the Hall of Fame pitcher who struck out 12 consecutive times one season—the official number of times he went to the plate. (On the mound he won four strikeout titles.)

78. Who was the 1958 first baseman who stole three bases, two of them home, in the same game? (A three-time .300 batter, he led the American League in triples in 1958.)

79. Who was the last switch-hitter in the American League to win the MVP award? (He was a pitcher.)

80. Name the player who hit safely in each of the 14 World Series games in which he participated. (His team won both of those Series in seven games.)

81. Which player got three or more hits in a record six consecutive games? (He won batting titles in three different decades.)

82. Who hit safely in 72 of 73 consecutive games? (He once had a 61-game batting streak in the Pacific Coast League.)

83. Who pitched a perfect game in his third major-league start? (He had a losing record in each of his eight years.)

84. Whose American League record for left-handed pitchers did Ron Guidry tie when he hurled nine shutouts in 1978? (He did it for the 1916 Red Sox.)
85. Who was the only pitcher to throw shutouts in both ends of a doubleheader? (He was also the only National League pitcher to lead his league in winning percentage three consecutive years.)
86. The only pitcher to strike out 10 consecutive batters, he registered those outs over the last 10 batters of a game. (He struck out 200 or more batters in a record nine consecutive seasons.) Who is he?
87. Who struck out a record 21 batters in a 16-inning game? (He posted a 19–29 eight-year record.)
88. The first pitcher to strike out 18 batters in a game lost that contest. (He won four consecutive strikeout crowns before World War II interrupted his career. When he returned from the war, he won three more consecutive strikeout crowns.) Who is he?
89. The first pitcher to strike out 19 batters in a game lost that contest. (Ron Swoboda hit two two-run homers to beat him, 4–3.) Who is he?
90. Who was the 1972 pitcher who threw 377 innings? (The following year, he both won and lost 20 games.)
91. Who was the only left-handed pitcher to win 30 games in a season? (He won 20 or more games in a season seven times.)
92. Name the "Ironman" who won three complete-

game doubleheaders in one month. (He also won more than 30 games in 1903 and 1904.)

93. Cy Young, who won a record 511 games, lost his last decision to a rookie who would go on to tie for the National League lead with 373 victories. (He won 30 games in each season from 1915 to 1917.) Who was that rookie?

94. Who was the only pitcher to lead both the National League and the American League in winning percentage? (He once won a record 41 games in one season.)

95. Who posted the highest career winning percentage for a pitcher with at least 150 decisions? (He was the MVP in the American League in 1943, when he was 20–4.)

96. Who was the pitcher who posted a record .718 winning percentage for relievers with at least 50 decisions? (He won two games and saved another for the Brooklyn Dodgers in the 1947 World Series. They lost the other four games.)

97. Whose 25–3 record set an all-time-high winning percentage (.893) for a 20-game winner? (He posted a league-leading 1.74 ERA that year.)

98. Who was the only pitcher to strike out 300 batters in his last season? (He won a league-leading 27 games, too.)

99. Only one pitcher has twice walked 200 batters in a season. (He was a flamethrower.) Who is he?

100. Who pitched all of his 1,050 games in relief? He set a record in doing so. (In the 1979 World Series he tied a record when he saved three games.)

BONUS QUESTION #1
Super Sleuths

Ty Cobb of the 1915 Tigers stole 96 bases, a record that stood for 47 years until a switch-hitting infielder broke it.

Since that time, three additional players have surpassed Cobb's total of 96 at least one time.

Rickey Henderson of the 1982 Oakland A's, of course, holds the all-time single-season mark with 130 stolen bases. Lou Brock of the 1974 Cardinals held the prior mark with 118 swiped bags. One other player, in addition to the switch-hitter, has topped the 100 mark—Vince Coleman, who stole a career-high 110 bases with the 1985 Cardinals, when he was a rookie.

But who was that switch-hitter whose 104 stolen bases in 1962 broke Cobb's longtime mark? He won six consecutive stolen base titles, from 1960 to 1965.

BONUS QUESTION #2
Batting Ch(u)mps

As a result of the Black Sox scandal of 1919, the owners replaced the old three-man National Commission that was headed by Ban Johnson, the former president of the American League, with an independent commissioner, Kenesaw Mountain Landis, a federal judge who once levied a high fine against the Standard Oil Company. The leaders of baseball wanted to win back the public trust.

The day after the eight players were acquitted by the grand jury in Chicago, Landis banned all of them from baseball for life. In effect, he said, "Regardless of the verdict of juries, no player who throws a ball game . . . will ever play professional baseball."

The players who were banned from the game for life were Chick Gandil, Swede Risberg, Fred McMullin, Buck Weaver, Joe Jackson, Happy Felsch, Eddie Cicotte, and Claude Williams.

What is not as well known is that around the same time, Landis also barred from baseball for life two former batting champs in the National League. One of them once won the Triple Crown. The other one is the only right-handed batter and left-handed fielder to win the batting crown. But they were dismissed from the game for allegedly placing bets on games in which they played.

Who were these two onetime stars whose light has dimmed over the years?

BONUS QUESTION #3
Surprise Starter

Manager Connie Mack of the 1929 Philadelphia Athletics had six pitchers who posted double-digit wins: George Earnshaw (24), Lefty Grove (20), Rube Walberg (18), Ed Rommel (12), Jack Quinn (12), and Bill Shores (11). But none of them pitched the opening game of that year's World Series against the Cubs.

Instead, Mack decided to go with a 35-year-old right-hander who would never again win a regular-season major-league game.

Mack's instincts were correct. The veteran of 15 major-league seasons—with a 166–166 career record—tantalized the hard-hitting Bruins batters with a variety of off-speed pitches and rolled to a 3–1 win behind a record 13 strikeouts, which stood until it was broken by Carl Erskine of the 1953 Brooklyn Dodgers, who mowed down 14 Yankees batters.

With the Red Sox in 1923, he no-hit the host Philadelphia Athletics, 4–0. Who was he?

Chapter One Answers

1. Sam Crawford (1899–1917 Reds and Tigers)
2. Stan Musial (Cardinals)
3. Warren Spahn (Boston Braves, Milwaukee Braves, Mets, and San Francisco Giants)
4. Eddie Sanicki
5. Walter Johnson (Senators)
6. Jimmie Foxx (Philadelphia Athletics, Red Sox, Cubs, and Phillies; Athletics and Red Sox)
7. Art Shamsky
8. Eddie Lopat (White Sox, Yankees, and Orioles)
9. Luke Appling (1936, 1943 White Sox)
10. Paul Waner (Pirates)
11. Ernie Lombardi (1938 Reds and 1942 Boston Braves)
12. Rogers Hornsby (.424 with 1924 Cardinals, .387 with 1928 Boston Braves, and .380 with 1929 Cubs)
13. Aaron Ward (1922 Yankees)
14. Willie Mays (1951 New York Giants and 1973 Mets; 1954 New York Giants and 1962 San Francisco Giants)
15. Duke Snider (1952, 1955 Brooklyn Dodgers)

16. Pete Runnels (1960 and 1962)
17. Carl Yastrzemski (1963, 1967, and 1968)
18. Joe DiMaggio (1937 and 1948 Yankees; 1939–40)
19. Bobby Richardson (1960 Yankees)
20. Sam Rice (1915–33 Senators and 1934 Indians)
21. Orel Hershiser (1986, 1989, and 1987 Los Angeles Dodgers; 1988 Dodgers and 1995 Indians)
22. Dwight Gooden (1984–85 Mets)
23. Andrew Dawson (Cubs; 1978 and 1985 Expos)
24. Howard Johnson (Mets)
25. Nick Esasky
26. Allie Reynolds (1947, 1949, and 1953 Yankees)
27. Willie McGee (1990 Cardinals and Oakland A's; 1985 Cardinals)
28. Steve Bedrosian (Atlanta Braves and Phillies)
29. Fernando Valenzuela (1981 Los Angeles Dodgers)
30. Fred Lynn (1975 Red Sox)
31. Jeff Russell (Rangers)
32. Don Mattingly (1987 Yankees)
33. George Bell (1988 Blue Jays)
34. Dave Stewart (1987–90 Oakland A's)
35. Wade Boggs (1986–89 Red Sox)
36. Bob Welch (1990 Oakland A's)
37. Mark McGwire (1987–90 Oakland A's)
38. Dave Winfield (Yankees)
39. Charlie Hough (1992 White Sox)
40. Pete Rose (1963–86 Reds, Phillies, and Expos)
41. Chuck Klein (1930 Phillies)
42. Willie Wilson (1985 Royals)
43. Ralph Kiner (1946–52 Pirates)
44. Gavvy Cravath (1919 Phillies; 1913–15 and 1917–19 Phillies)

45. Johnny Bench (1970 and 1972 Reds)
46. Rocky Colavito (1959 Indians, for Harvey Kuenn of the Tigers; 1959 Indians)
47. Wally Pipp (1916–17)
48. Hank Greenberg (1940 and 1946 Tigers; 1937 Tigers)
49. Reggie Jackson (Oakland A's, Yankees, and Angels)
50. Darrell Evans (1985 Tigers; 1973 Atlanta Braves and 1985 Tigers)
51. Johnny Mize (51 and 42 for the 1947 New York Giants)
52. Willie Mays (24 with the 1955 New York Giants and 34 with the 1965 San Francisco Giants)
53. Babe Ruth (1935 Boston Braves)
54. Joe Jackson (1911 Indians; Ty Cobb of the Tigers, who batted .420, copped the crown; 1920 White Sox.)
55. Rogers Hornsby (1921–25 Cardinals)
56. Eddie Collins (1906–30 Philadelphia Athletics and White Sox)
57. Bob Watson (1977 Astros and 1979 Red Sox; Astros and Yankees)
58. Honus Wagner (Pirates)
59. Tony Fernandez (Blue Jays)
60. Tony Gwynn (.313 with the 1988 Padres; 1994 Padres)
61. Walter Johnson (1925 Senators)
62. Al Simmons (1930–31 Philadelphia Athletics; 1924–34 Philadelphia Athletics and White Sox)
63. Rod Carew (1972 Twins)

64. Al Oliver (Expos; Pirates, Rangers, Expos, and San Francisco Giants and Phillies)
65. Ty Cobb (1920–28 Tigers and Philadelphia Athletics; 1907–15 Tigers)
66. Matty Alou of the 1966 Pirates and Felipe Alou of the 1966 Atlanta Braves
67. Lou Boudreau (1944 and 1948 Indians)
68. Norm Cash (1961 Tigers)
69. Harmon Killebrew (1964 and 1969 Twins)
70. Heinie Zimmerman (98 with the 1912 Cubs)
71. Willie Mays
72. Mickey Mantle
73. Joe Jackson (1911 Indians)
74. George Stirnweiss
75. Joe DiMaggio (418)
76. Ted Williams
77. Sandy Koufax (1955 Brooklyn Dodgers)
78. Vic Power (Kansas City A's)
79. Vida Blue (1971 Oakland A's)
80. Roberto Clemente (1960 and 1971 Pirates)
81. George Brett (1976 Royals; 1976, 1980, and 1990 Royals)
82. Joe DiMaggio (1941 Yankees)
83. Charlie Robertson (1922 White Sox)
84. Babe Ruth
85. Ed Reulbach (1908 Cubs; 1906–8 Cubs)
86. Tom Seaver (1970 Mets)
87. Tom Cheney (1962 Senators)
88. Bob Feller (1938 Indians)
89. Steve Carlton (1969 Cardinals)
90. Wilbur Wood (White Sox)

91. Lefty Grove (31 with the 1931 Philadelphia Athletics)
92. Joe McGinnity (1903 New York Giants; August)
93. Grover Alexander (1911 Phillies)
94. Jack Chesbro (1901–2 Pirates and 1904 Yankees; 1904 Yankees)
95. Spud Chandler (.717 with the 1937–47 Yankees)
96. Hugh Casey (1935–49 Reds, Brooklyn Dodgers, Pirates, and Yankees)
97. Ron Guidry (1978 Yankees)
98. Sandy Koufax (1966 Los Angeles Dodgers)
99. Nolan Ryan (202 with 1972 California Angels and 204 with 1977 Angels)
100. Kent Tekulve (1974–89 Pirates, Phillies, and Reds; Pirates)

Chapter One Score

Number of Hits (Correct Answers)   _____
Number of At Bats (Questions)   _____
Season Batting Average   _____

Chapter Two: Part One

Present-Day National League Players Lenny, Ozzie, and the Straw

1. Whose first-year average of .318 was the highest by any National League Rookie of the Year winner since the honor was initiated in 1947? (He was also the first winner to drive home 100 or more runs, 112, in a season.)
2. Which 1994 San Francisco pitcher hit .354, the highest average by a Giants moundsman since Joe Genewich hit .375 in 1929?
3. Who in 1992 became only the second player in history to cop four-base crowns in both leagues?
4. Identify the outfielder who in 1992 scored 143 runs, the most in the National League since Chuck Klein of the 1932 Phillies plated 152.

5. Who in 1993 became the first Reds pitcher since Ewell Blackwell in 1947 to lead the league in strikeouts?
6. Name the player who tied two major-league records when he hit four home runs and drove home 12 runs in a 1993 game against the Reds.
7. Which player, in addition to Rick Sutcliffe, Fernando Valenzuela, and Steve Sax, was one of four Los Angeles Dodgers to win consecutive Rookie of the Year awards from 1979 to 1982?
8. Which player, in addition to Eric Karros and Mike Piazza, was one of three Los Angeles Dodgers to win consecutive Rookie of the Year awards from 1992 to 1994?
9. Who in 1990 tied Maury Wills's National League record of six consecutive stolen base titles?
10. Who in 1994 became only the fourth hurler since 1900 to record more wins (14) than walks (13) in a minimum of 150 innings? (He set the modern-day record by granting just 0.7 walks per nine innings.)
11. Identify the youngest defending batting champ (.330 in 1992) to be traded.
12. What Phillies infielder had a 66-game errorless streak in 1993?
13. Whose 40 home runs by the end of July in 1994 set a league mark?
14. Who became the first player to suit up for clubs in two professional sports on the same day?
15. Who is the only shortstop in the last 40 years to bat better than .300 in five consecutive (1989–93) years?

16. Name the 1993 pitcher who became the first National League moundsman to win 20 games three years in a row since Ferguson Jenkins of the 1967–72 Cubs won 20 games six years in succession?

17. Which Bruin became the first 30–30 player in the Cubs' history?

18. Name the first player in history to be selected to the All-Star Team at both catcher (1991) and second base (1992).

19. Who in 1994 became baseball's all-time assist leader, breaking Luis Aparicio's mark?

20. Whose 35 home runs in his rookie year were second only to Wally Berger's (1930 Boston Braves) and Frank Robinson's (1956 Reds) 38?

21. What player has hit .300 for 14 consecutive seasons, the longest string since Stan Musial topped the .300 mark for 16 successive seasons?

22. Who became the youngest catcher to call a no-hitter since Ted Simmons received Bob Gibson's in 1971?

23. Identify the 1993 Atlanta Braves shortstop who became the first club player at that position to bat .300 (.305) since Alvin Dark stroked .322 in 1948.

24. Who became the first player since Carl Yastrzemski of the 1967 Red Sox to finish first or second in his league in batting average (.368), home runs (39), runs (104), and RBIs (116)?

25. Identify the Cardinal who went to the plate 416 official times in 1993 without grounding into a double play.

26. What outfielder reached the 30-30 mark for the third time in 1995?

27. Name the player who has won three MVP awards.

28. Identify the right-handed batter who averaged 34 home runs per year from 1990 to 1994.

29. Who in 1990 became the youngest Dodgers pitcher to win 20 games since Ralph Branca did it with Brooklyn in 1947?

30. Identify the 1994 rookie who became just the fifth player in major-league history to begin the season in the minors, yet be selected to the All-Star Team.

31. Name the player who has a father and a grandfather who played in the majors.

32. Whose 53 saves in 1993 set a league record?

33. Who was the only pitcher to save 45 games in a season in both leagues?

34. Name the youngest hurler in Braves history (23) to record 50 wins.

35. Whose 17 home runs in 1994 all came off right-handed pitching?

36. Which player has batted .320, hit six home runs, and driven home 11 runs in 13 World Series games?

37. Name the Cub who 12 times has had consecutive-game hitting streaks in the double digits?

38. Who in 1987 hit a record-tying three grand slams in one month?

39. Identify the player who won the league batting title while grounding into a loop-high 20 double plays.

40. Name the infielder who started in a record 10 consecutive All-Star Games at his position.
41. Who became the first Dodger to hit 20 or more home runs in each of his first two seasons?
42. Name the onetime American League left-handed slugger who in 1993 slammed 34 home runs for the Padres in his first National League season.
43. Who along with his father is a partner in the all-time father-son career home run record? (Going into the 1996 season, they had combined for 624.)
44. Identify the former Met who two times hit a club-high 39 home runs in a season.
45. Whose 18 strikeouts in one game tied Sandy Koufax's team mark?
46. Who has hit .300 with the Indians, the San Francisco Giants, and the Los Angeles Dodgers?
47. Name the National League catcher who turned in a .999 fielding percentage in 1992.
48. Whose 1.56 ERA in 1994 was a record 1.09 lower than that of the next major-league pitcher?
49. What pitcher won the Cy Young Award, the National League Championship Series MVP award, and the World Series MVP award in 1988? (He batted .356 in 1993.)
50. Whose .370 average in 1993 was the highest league mark by a right-handed batter since Joe Medwick of the 1937 Cardinals hit .374?

Chapter Two: Part-One Answers

1. Mike Piazza (1993 Los Angeles Dodgers)
2. Mark Portugal
3. Fred McGriff (Atlanta Braves, 1989 Blue Jays)
4. Lenny Dykstra
5. Jose Rijo
6. Mark Whiten (Cardinals)
7. Steve Howe (1980)
8. Raul Mondesi (1994)
9. Vince Coleman (1985–90 Cardinals)
10. Bret Saberhagen (Mets)
11. Gary Sheffield (Padres to Marlins, 24)
12. Mickey Morandini
13. Matt Williams (San Francisco Giants)
14. Deion Sanders (1992 Atlanta Falcons and Atlanta Braves)
15. Barry Larkin (Reds)
16. Tom Glavine (1991–93 Atlanta Braves)
17. Sammy Sosa (1993)
18. Craig Biggio (Astros)
19. Ozzie Smith (Cardinals)
20. Mike Piazza (1993 Los Angeles Dodgers)
21. Tony Gwynn (1983–95 Padres)

22. Javier Lopez (1994 Atlanta Braves, 24)
23. Jeff Blauser
24. Jeff Bagwell (Astros)
25. Ray Lankford
26. Barry Bonds (1990 and 1992 Pirates; 1995 San Francisco Giants)
27. Barry Bonds (1990 and 1992 Pirates; 1993 San Francisco Giants)
28. Matt Williams (San Francisco Giants)
29. Ramon Martinez (22)
30. John Hudek (Astros)
31. Bret Boone (Bob and Ray)
32. Randy Myers (Cubs)
33. Bryan Harvey (46 with the 1991 Angels and 45 with the 1993 Marlins)
34. Steve Avery (1993)
35. Ryan Klesko (Atlanta Braves)
36. Lenny Dykstra (1986 Mets and 1993 Phillies)
37. Mark Grace
38. Eric Davis (Reds)
39. Tony Gwynn (1994 Padres)
40. Ozzie Smith (Cardinals shortstop)
41. Eric Karros (1992–93)
42. Phil Plantier
43. Barry Bonds (Bobby)
44. Darryl Strawberry (1987–88)
45. Ramon Martinez (1990)
46. Brett Butler
47. Tom Pagnozzi (Cardinals)
48. Greg Maddux (Atlanta Braves)
49. Orel Hershiser (Los Angeles Dodgers)
50. Andres Galarraga (Rockies)

Chapter Two: Part Two

Present-Day
American League Players
Kirby, Kenny, and Big Mac

1. Who tied a record when he hit a home run in each of eight consecutive games? (He tied Dale Long of the 1956 Pirates and Don Mattingly of the 1987 Yankees.)
2. Whose father was an outstanding wide receiver for Notre Dame and the Los Angeles Rams?
3. Which pitcher won back-to-back Cy Young awards?
4. Identify the pitcher who threw a perfect game in 1994.
5. What Brewer led his team in homers from 1991 to 1994?
6. Name the pitcher who was 35–10 in 1993 and 1994.
7. Identify the last player before Albert Belle to hit 50 home runs in a season.

8. Which Oriole has been the only Bird to win two MVP awards?

9. Which Oriole stole 31 bases in 32 attempts in 1994, the best mark in history up to that time for a base sleuth with at least 25 steals in one season?

10. Name the 1994 shortstop who converted the tenth unassisted triple play in history.

11. Which player was a .259 hitter in six seasons in the National League before he became a .335 batter in his first two years in the American League?

12. Who holds the league record for hitting three home runs in a game five times?

13. Name the first back-to-back MVP winner in the American League since Roger Maris of the 1960–61 Yankees.

14. Name the Oriole who hit a career-high 39 home runs in 1995.

15. Which Rookie of the Year winner was sent to the minors early in the following season?

16. What Brewers pitcher once won 10 games in a row?

17. Which pitcher has won six Gold Glove awards?

18. Who in 1996 became the first player on his team to hit 25 or more homers for seven consecutive years?

19. Name today's only pitcher to strike out 300 batters in a season.

20. Who set a Blue Jays record when he reached base in 37 consecutive games in 1994?

21. Identify the 25-year-old catcher who played in five All-Star Games in his first six years in the majors.

22. Who in addition to Wade Boggs is the only American League player to win two batting titles?

23. Who became the only player in major-league

history to bat .300 or better with 20 home runs, 100 RBIs, 100 walks, and 100 runs for five consecutive seasons?

24. Who in 1995 became the first Yankee since Bobby Murcer to hit for the cycle?

25. Name the latest of six pitchers to win at least 100 games in each league.

26. Who was the 1993–94 White Sox pitcher who went 24–7 in his first two years in the majors?

27. Identify the former White Sox pitcher who won 20 games in back-to-back years with the Pale Hose.

28. Who set the major-league record for consecutive successful save opportunities (38) in 1995?

29. Which Orioles catcher became one of only five receivers in league history to hit .300 and 25 home runs in the same season?

30. One other present-day catcher belongs to the above group. Who is he?

31. Identify the all-time career home run king at shortstop in the junior circuit.

32. What player was drafted by an owner who admired his Little League play?

33. Name the player who had a fly ball bounce off his head and over the fence for a home run against Cleveland in 1993.

34. He averaged 38 home runs a season from 1990 to 1994, but he didn't steal a base during that time. Who is he?

35. Name the shortstop who fielded a record .996 in 1990.

36. Identify the player who has hit more home runs in one season than any other White Sox player.

37. Who is the only Indian to hit 30-plus home runs for four straight seasons?

38. Who in 1987 became only the second unanimous Rookie of The Year choice?

39. What player saw his home run production fall from 46 in 1993 to 19 in 1994?

40. Whose 42 steals in 1994 were the most by a Red Sox since Tommy Harper of the 1973 Red Sox racked up a club-record 54?

41. What 1994 player was suspended for six games for corking his bat?

42. Whose Gold Glove awards in 1994 and 1995 were his first two over a 15-year career? (He's always had some silver in his bat.)

43. Identify the only player to win MVP, All-Star Game MVP, and the Cy Young Award in the same season.

44. Who in 1993 almost became the first American League catcher to bat .300 and hit 30 home runs?

45. Name the Mariner who in 1993 hit a grand slam in back-to-back games.

46. Identify the player who stroked 200 or more hits in a record seven consecutive seasons.

47. Name the Yankee whose .359 batting average was the highest by a pinstriper since Mickey Mantle of the 1957 Bombers hit .365.

48. Who moved into the select 3,000 Hit Club in 1995?

49. What player titled his autobiography *I Love This Game*?

50. Who has hit home runs from both sides of the plate a record 11 times?

Chapter Two: Part-Two Answers

1. Ken Griffey Jr. (1993 Mariners)
2. J. T. Snow (Jack)
3. Roger Clemens (1986–87 Red Sox)
4. Kenny Rogers (Rangers)
5. Greg Vaughn
6. Jimmy Key (Yankees)
7. Cecil Fielder (51 with the 1990 Tigers)
8. Cal Ripken (1983 and 1991)
9. Brady Anderson
10. John Valentin (Red Sox)
11. Paul O'Neill (Yankees)
12. Joe Carter
13. Frank Thomas (1993–94 White Sox)
14. Rafael Palmeiro
15. Bob Hamelin (1994–95 Royals)
16. Cal Eldred (1992)
17. Mark Langston
18. Cecil Fielder (1990–95 Tigers)
19. Randy Johnson (308 with the 1993 Mariners)
20. Joe Carter
21. Ivan Rodriguez (Rangers)
22. Edgar Martinez (1992 and 1995 Mariners)

23. Frank Thomas (1991–95 White Sox)
24. Tony Fernandez
25. Dennis Martinez (Indians)
26. Jason Bere
27. Jack McDowell (1992–93)
28. Jose Mesa (Indians)
29. Chris Hoiles (1993)
30. Mike Stanley (1993 Yankees)
31. Cal Ripken (327, going into the 1996 season)
32. Harold Baines (Bill Veeck)
33. Jose Canseco (Rangers)
34. Cecil Fielder (Tigers)
35. Cal Ripken (Orioles)
36. Frank Thomas (41 in 1993)
37. Albert Belle (1992–95)
38. Mark McGwire (Carlton Fisk of the 1972 Red Sox was the first.)
39. Juan Gonzalez (Rangers)
40. Otis Nixon
41. Albert Belle (Indians)
42. Wade Boggs (Yankees)
43. Roger Clemens (1986 Red Sox)
44. Chris Hoiles (.310 and 29)
45. Mike Blowers
46. Wade Boggs (1983–89 Red Sox)
47. Paul O'Neill (1994)
48. Eddie Murray (Orioles)
49. Kirby Puckett
50. Eddie Murray

Chapter Two Score

Number of Hits (Correct Answers)   ————

Number of At Bats (Questions)   ————

Season Batting Average   ————

BONUS QUESTION #4
The Streakers

Cal Ripken of the Orioles became a baseball immortal on September 6, 1995, when he broke Lou Gehrig's long and celebrated record of 2,130 consecutive games played. Going into the 1996 season, Ripken's record was 2,153 consecutive games.

Gehrig's former record streak began in 1925 when he pinch-hit one day for Pee Wee Wanninger. It ended when he took himself out of the lineup because of sickness in 1939.

Who was the former teammate whose prior major-league streak Gehrig broke? A .249 career hitter, he played 13 years at shortstop in the major leagues.

BONUS QUESTION #5
The Deacon

Only one manager has led three different teams in the same league into the World Series.

He skippered Pittsburgh to a seven-game victory in the 1925 World Series, its first title since 1909. But unbelievably, he was fired from that post after he directed the Pirates to a third-place finish in 1926.

Two years later, he was once again a major-league manager, leading St. Louis to its second pennant in three years. But after his club got swept by the Yankees in the World Series and got off to a fourth-place start the next year, he was demoted by owner Sam Breadon of the Cardinals to the helm of Rochester in the International League.

The following season, he was back in the majors again, leading a perennial second-division club, the Braves, to two fourth-place finishes in eight years.

In 1938, he switched teams to the Reds and led them to back-to-back pennants the following two years, losing the World Series in four games to the 1939 Yankees but copping the Fall Classic in seven games from the 1940 Tigers.

In 1937, his last season with that "perennial second-division club," he was named Major League Manager of the Year by *Sporting News* for skillfully leading a mediocre team to a fifth-place finish. On that team, however, he developed two 30-year-old rookie pitchers, Lou Fette and Jim Turner, into 20-game winners.

Who was that "deacon" of National League managers?

BONUS QUESTION #6
Beating the Depression

In 1930, during the early days of the Depression, the owners pumped more life into the baseball than they ever had before. Sensing that the fans wanted to see more hitting, they lured them to the parks with the livelier ball.

The experiment was super successful in the National League, which drew a record 5.5 million paying customers, half a million more than the previous year.

Hack Wilson of the Cubs hit 56 home runs, a National League record, and he drove home 190 runs, a major-league mark. Both records still stand.

The New York Giants as a team hit a record .319. First baseman Bill Terry became the last National League player to hit .400 (.401), lashing 254 hits, which tied the league record that had been set the year before.

Six teams—the Giants, Dodgers, Phillies, Pirates, Cubs, and Cardinals—posted team averages that were over .300. In 1968, to point out a comparison, only six players in the senior circuit hit over .300.

The Phillies, who finished last in the league standings, batted .315 as a club, all-time runner-up to the Giants record .319. Right fielder Chuck Klein batted .386. His counterpart in left field hit .383. The year before, he had batted a league-leading .398, just one hit shy of .400, and he had collected a league-record 254 safeties.

A decade earlier, he had split two decisions in parts of four years with the Yankees and the Red Sox. Who was that player who switched to the outfield and found greener pastures in the National League?

Chapter Three

Allie, Sandy, and the Moose

1. Two Yankees infielders batted better than .400 in the 1978 World Series. Who filled in for the injured Willie Randolph and batted .438? (He batted .161 lifetime.)
2. Name the player who batted .417 and won the MVP award in the 1978 World Series.
3. Five Pirates ended up with double-figure base hits in the 1979 World Series against the Orioles. (Two of them had 12.) Who was the left-handed slugger?
4. Who was the right-handed-hitting infielder? (He is a present-day manager.)
5. A Phillies pitcher proved to be prominent in the climactic games of the 1980 World Series against

the Royals. (He won game five and saved game six.) Who is he?

6. The MVP of the 1986 World Series, a free agent after the Fall Classic, wasn't signed by his club for 1987. (He is a present-day manager, too.) Who is he?

7. Name the first player to perform with three different world-title teams. (He threw "bullets" for the 1913 Philadelphia Athletics, the 1918 Red Sox, and the 1923 Yankees.)

8. The second person to perform for three world-title teams, he was the first man to play with Fall Classic champs in both leagues. (Name the onetime member of the "$100,000 Infield.")

9. Name the Cardinals rookie catcher who got four hits in a World Series game. (He later made a living telling Yogi Berra jokes.)

10. He was the only pitcher to register five decisions in one World Series, winning three games and losing two. (Also, he was the only hurler to twice pitch back-to-back contests in the same Series.) Who was he?

11. Who was the Yankees pitcher who retired the first 22 Pirates he faced in a World Series game? (He won all five of his Fall Classic decisions.)

12. Identify the 31-game winner in 1910 who won five games and batted .333 in total World Series play. (He was called "Colby Jack.")

13. Lou Brock of the Cardinals was thrown out at the plate, trying to score a key run in game five of the 1968 World Series, by what Tiger left fielder? (He hit 325 lifetime home runs.)

14. Who was the National League pitcher who granted only one run in 25⅓ innings of Fall Classic competition? (He hurled against the Orioles, Red Sox, and Yankees in the 1972, 1975, and 1976 World Series.)

15. Who was the first pitcher to win the final game of two consecutive Fall Classics? (He did it with the winning 1921–22 New York Giants.)

16. Who was the last pitcher to win the final game of two consecutive World Series? (He started the opening game of four World Series in the post–World War II era.)

17. Who was the .257 lifetime hitter who batted .500 in the 1953 World Series? (His 12 hits were a record for a six-game Classic.)

18. What Yankees pitcher copped the last game of the 1927 World Series as a starter and the final game of the 1932 Fall Classic as a reliever? (In 1927 he won 13 games and saved 13 contests out of the bull pen.)

19. Who was the pitcher of the 1920s who won both the sixth and the seventh game of a World Series? (The two-time 20-game winner did it for the Pirates.)

20. Name the Brooklyn Dodgers pitcher who hit into a record five outs in two consecutive at bats in a World Series game. (One of those times, he hit into the World Series' only triple play.)

21. Who was the Yankees standout who performed in a record 30 consecutive World Series games, played in five consecutive years? In 1962 he led

the American League in at bats with 692 and in hits with 209.)

22. What player appeared in a record nine World Series games as a pinch runner? (He never had an at bat, however.)

23. Whose 25 hits in two consecutive World Series set a record? (He is one of only three players to get 13 hits in a Fall Classic.)

24. Name the present-day American Leaguer who is the only player to get five hits in a World Series game.

25. What National League player drove home a record six runs in one World Series as a pinch-hitter? (He batted .341 with 15 home runs for the 1954 New York Giants. Careerwise, he batted .253.)

26. One Yankees catcher was eligible for 37 World Series contests, but played in only one of them. (In his eight full years as a backup to Yogi Berra, the Yankees won seven pennants and six world titles.) Who is he?

27. Name the two-time home run champ who tied a major-league record in 1992 when he received seven consecutive bases on balls.

28. What Hall of Fame infielder played in his two World Series 14 years apart? (His first team, the Boston Braves, swept the Series; his second team, the Cardinals, got swept.)

29. Name the 1970 Reds pitcher who didn't allow an earned run in four World Series relief appearances. (Overall, in 14 World Series games, his ERA was 1.33.)

30. Who was the last Cubs pitcher to win a World Series game? (He also won a Fall Classic contest with the 1943 Yankees.)

31. Whose only World Series victory was a three-hit shutout in game seven of the 1956 Fall Classic? (From 1955 to 1958 he pitched in eight postseason games and chalked up a 1.89 ERA.)

32. Name the 1929–30 Philadelphia Athletics pitcher who hurled consecutive starting games in back-to-back World Series. (He was 4–3 with a 1.58 ERA in the 1929–31 Fall Classics.)

33. What player hit into a record three double plays in one World Series game? (A Hall of Famer, he was a rookie that year.)

34. One Hall of Famer hit into a record seven double plays in World Series competition. Who was he? (He hit eight home runs in postseason play.)

35. Identify the pitcher who won his only opening-game start in the World Series, 1–0. (He played on a record six of six winners in the Fall Classic.)

36. Who was the only pitcher to lose two 1–0 games in the World Series? (Three times this 327-game winner lost by shutout in the Fall Classic.)

37. In his first World Series start, he struck out 11 batters but lost to Allie Reynolds of the Yankees, 1–0. (Tommy Henrich's home run in the bottom of the ninth inning beat him.) Who is he?

38. In 1956, this future World Series MVP struck out 11 batters in a 10-inning World Series game but lost to Clem Labine, 1–0, (Jackie Robinson's

single, misplayed by left fielder Enos Slaughter, beat him.) What is his name?

39. Reach back for the name of the pitcher who struck out 12 batters in a 12-inning World Series game against the New York Giants, but lost 4–3. (In the final game of the 1924 World Series, he won in relief, 4–3, in a contest that went 12 innings.)

40. Name the Yankees pitcher of the 1930s and 1940s who won seven of nine decisions in World Series play. (He won six straight decisions between 1937 and 1942.)

41. Identify the Yankees hurler of the 1940s and 1950s who won seven of nine World Series verdicts. (He also played in a record six of six winning Fall Classics.)

42. Who was the youngest manager (27) of a World Series winner? (He was a playing manager who later, with another team, copped a Fall Classic as a bench manager.)

43. Name the youngest manager (26) of a World Series team. (He later won a pennant as a bench manager, too.)

44. Two pitchers hit a record two home runs in World Series play. (The National League pitcher also logged a 1.89 ERA in three Fall Classics.) Who was the National League pitcher?

45. Who was the American League hurler who homered twice? (They were the only two hits he got in four World Series during the 1960s and 1970s.)

46. Who was John McGraw's relief pitcher with the

New York Giants who struck out a National League—record 10 batters in a World Series game? (His brother pitched on the same team.)

47. Who was the youngest pitcher (19) to hurl in the World Series? (His brother won three batting titles.)

48. Who outpitched Ron Darling of the Mets in a 1986 World Series game, 1–0? (He was 3–0 in postseason play that year with the Red Sox.)

49. In game four of the 1966 World Series, he outdueled Don Drysdale of the Los Angeles Dodgers, 1–0. (Frank Robinson's home run made the difference.) Who is he?

50. Who eked out a 1–0 decision over the Los Angeles Dodgers' Claude Osteen in game three of the 1966 World Series? (He was only 21 years old.)

51. In game three of the 1963 World Series, he outdueled Jim Bouton of the Yankees, 1–0. (Later, he would become the second and last pitcher to both win and lose a 1–0 decision in Fall Classic competition.) Who was he?

52. Identify the Yankee hurler who outpitched Jack Sanford of the San Francisco Giants in game seven of the 1962 World Series, 1–0. (Two years before, he had lost a seventh game.)

53. Name the first baseman who was a pivotal part of four world title teams with the Yankees and one with the Los Angeles Dodgers. (He batted .385 with the Dodgers against his old teammates.)

54. Identify the player who performed on one

world title team with the Senators (1924) and another with the Tigers (1935). (He won a batting title with Washington in 1928, and he delivered the Series-winning hit with Detroit in 1935.)

55. Who was the player who performed on three consecutive pennant winners with the 1929–31 Philadelphia Athletics and back-to-back flag winners with the 1934–35 Tigers? (As a playing manager, he led Detroit to its first world title in 1935.)

56. Name the second baseman who played on world championship clubs with the Yankees and the Indians. (He won the MVP award in 1942.)

57. Who started the opening game of the World Series for the world title Reds one year and the world championship Yankees the next? (In his first opening game start, he beat the Yankees.)

58. What slugger of the 1960s played on two world title teams with the Yankees and one with the Cardinals? (He won back-to-back MVP awards in 1960 and 1961.)

59. Who excelled in left field for the Brooklyn Dodgers in game six of the 1947 World Series, denying Joe DiMaggio's bid for a three-run, game-tying homer? (He was inserted in that inning as a substitute outfielder.)

60. Name the player who excelled at second base for the Yankees in the 1952 World Series against the Brooklyn Dodgers. (His knee-high catch of

Jackie Robinson's pop-up saved the seventh game and the Series for the Yankees.)

61. Which left fielder's catch of Yogi Berra's slicing fly ball in game seven of the 1955 World Series led to a pivotal double play in Brooklyn's 2–0 victory over the Yankees? (He batted .333 with a homer and three RBIs.)

62. Whose running catch of Gil Hodges' long blast in game five of the 1956 World Series saved Don Larsen's perfect game for the Yankees against the Dodgers? (He hit a home run off losing pitcher Sal Maglie in the 2–0 New York win.)

63. Which center fielder for the 1960 Pirates made a couple of scintillating catches in the World Series? (Later, he managed the Yankees, the team he helped beat in 1960.)

64. Identify the player who starred in right field for the Mets in the 1969 World Series. (In game four he robbed Brooks Robinson of what appeared to be a game-winning triple.)

65. Who excelled in center field for the Mets in the 1969 World Series? (In game three he made two spectacular catches, one that took a triple away from Elrod Hendricks and another that denied Paul Blair a three-base hit.)

66. Name the only player of a losing team to win the MVP Award in the World Series. (He hit a grand slam, drove home a record 12 runs, and batted .391.)

67. Two pitchers won the World Series MVP Award twice. One led his team to victory in 1963 and

1965. (He won four of his five decisions in those two Series.) Who is he?

68. The other led his team to victory in 1964 and 1967. (After losing his first verdict, he won five consecutive decisions in those two Classics.) Who is he?

69. Identify the only nonpitcher to win the World Series MVP award twice. (He did it with two different teams.)

70. Who was the first relief pitcher to win the World Series MVP award? (He won two games and saved two others in 1959.)

71. Who was the manager of the 1948–49 Red Sox when they lost the pennant on the last day of the season? (He once won a pennant with the Cubs.)

72. Identify the person who was the first manager to win back-to-back World Series. (He was also the first and last skipper to win a Fall Classic with the Cubs.)

73. Who, in addition to John McGraw, has been the only Giants manager to win back-to-back pennants? (He was a .341 lifetime hitter.)

74. Which manager led his team to three consecutive pennants during World War II and then another club to a flag after the war? (An outfielder, he batted .345 for the winning Cardinals in the 1926 World Series.)

75. Who was the manager who won back-to-back pennants with the Brooklyn Dodgers and then got released because he wanted a two-year con-

tract? (He lost both World Series to the Yankees.)

76. Who, in addition to John McGraw, was the only National League field leader to win back-to-back pennants more than once? (He had only one at bat in the majors, with the 1936 Cardinals.)

77. Name the last National League manager to win back-to-back world titles. (He also won another world title with a team in the opposite league.)

78. Who was the first manager to lose three consecutive World Series? (This .312 lifetime hitter never won one.)

79. Two managers have led their clubs to at least four consecutive world titles. (One of them never played in the major leagues.) Who was he?

80. The other one won a record five consecutive world titles. (He hit .393 in three World Series with the Brooklyn Dodgers and the New York Giants.) Who was he?

81. What manager led his team to world titles in his first two years as a skipper? (Eligible for six World Series as a player, he got only two at bats.)

82. Who led the 1967 Red Sox, the 1972–73 Oakland A's, and the 1984 Padres to pennants? (The two Oakland clubs won world titles.)

83. Identify the last American League manager to win three consecutive pennants. (He now manages in the National League.)

84. Who was the last playing manager in the National league to lead his team to a world title?

(Basically a second baseman, he batted .294 in eight World Series and .316 over a 16-year career.)

85. Who was the playing manager who hit a dramatic home run in the closing days of the 1938 season? (His club got swept by the Yankees in that year's World Series.)

86. Who was the pitcher who threw the historic 61st home run pitch to Roger Maris in 1961? (He later lost 20 games for the 1964 Mets.)

87. Name the last Red Sox manager to win a world title. Later, when he was a general manager, his team, not the Red Sox, won 14 pennants and 10 world titles.)

88. Who was the only St. Louis Browns manager to lead his team to a pennant? (A 20-year catcher with four clubs, he had two brothers, including a Hall of Famer, who played in the majors.)

89. Who was the last manager to wear street clothes to lead his club to a pennant? (He twice succeeded Leo Durocher as a manager.)

90. Identify the only manager to lead the Phillies to a world title. (He later managed the Mets.)

91. Name Ty Cobb's most successful pupil as the manager of the Tigers. (The "pupil" won four batting titles.)

92. Reach back and identify the last White Sox manager to lead Chicago to a world title. (He never played in the majors. His nickname was Pants.)

93. The last Yankees manager to lead the Bombers to a world title (1978) was a Hall of Fame

pitcher. (He once won two games for a club that won its last world title.)

94. Who at 39 became the oldest player to win the regular-season MVP award? (He hit 475 lifetime home runs.)

95. Who was the relief pitcher from 1958 and 1959 who won a record 22 consecutive games? (In 1960 he saved a record three games in one World Series.)

96. In 1955 he became the only pitcher to win the ERA title with a last-place club. (Though he led his league, with 22 wins in 1958, he dropped both of his decisions in the 1960 World Series, and he ended his career with 33 more losses, 230, than wins, 197.) Who is he?

97. Who holds the American League single-season record for most stolen bases (20) without being caught stealing?

98. A lifetime .344 hitter, this left-handed batter averaged more than 100 walks a season. (At the age of 38, he drew an American League–record 33 intentional bases on balls.) Who is he?

99. Two players have won the Triple Crown twice. Name the .359 lifetime hitter who won it in both 1922 and 1925.

100. Name the .344 lifetime hitter who won it in both 1942 and 1947. (He didn't win the MVP award in either year.)

Chapter Three Answers

1. Brian Doyle
2. Bucky Dent
3. Willie Stargell
4. Phil Garner
5. Tug McGraw
6. Ray Knight
7. "Bullet" Joe Bush
8. John "Stuffy" McInnis (1911 and 1913 Philadelphia Athletics, 1918 Red Sox, and 1925 Pirates)
9. Joe Garagiola (1946 Cardinals)
10. Deacon Phillippe (1903 Pirates)
11. Herb Pennock (1927)
12. Jack Coombs (Philadelphia Athletics)
13. Willie Horton
14. Jack Billingham (Reds)
15. Art Nehf
16. Allie Reynolds (1952–53 Yankees; 1949, 1951–53 Yankees)
17. Billy Martin (Yankees)
18. Wilcy Moore
19. Ray Kremer (1925)
20. Clarence Mitchell (1920)

21. Bobby Richardson (1960–64 Yankees)
22. Allan Lewis (1972–73 Oakland A's)
23. Lou Brock (1967–68 Cardinals; Bobby Richardson, 1964 Yankees, and Marty Barrett, 1986 Red Sox, got 13 hits in a series, too.)
24. Paul Molitor (1982 Brewers)
25. Dusty Rhodes (1954 New York Giants)
26. Charlie Silvera
27. Jose Canseco (1988, 1991 Oakland A's)
28. Walter "Rabbit" Maranville (1914 and 1928)
29. Clay Carroll
30. Hank Borowy (1945)
31. Johnny Kucks (Yankees)
32. George Earnshaw
33. Willie Mays (1951 New York Giants)
34. Joe DiMaggio (Yankees)
35. Vic Raschi (1950 Yankees)
36. Eddie Plank (1905 and 1914 Philadelphia Athletics)
37. Don Newcombe (1949 Brooklyn Dodgers)
38. Bob Turley (Yankees; 1958)
39. Walter Johnson (Senators)
40. Red Ruffing
41. Allie Reynolds
42. Bucky Harris (1924 Senators and 1947 Yankees)
43. Joe Cronin (1933 Senators and 1946 Red Sox)
44. Bob Gibson (1967–68 Cardinals)
45. Dave McNally (1969–70 Orioles)
46. Jesse Barnes (1921; Virgil)
47. Ken Brett (1967 Red Sox; George)
48. Bruce Hurst
49. Dave McNally (Orioles)

50. Wally Bunker
51. Don Drysdale (Los Angeles Dodgers)
52. Ralph Terry
53. Bill Skowron (1956, 1958, 1961–62; 1963)
54. Leon "Goose" Goslin
55. Mickey Cochrane
56. Joe Gordon (1938–39, 1941, 1943 Yankees; 1948 Indians)
57. Don Gullett
58. Roger Maris (1961–62 and 1967)
59. Al Gionfriddo
60. Billy Martin
61. Sandy Amoros
62. Mickey Mantle
63. Bill Virdon
64. Ron Swoboda
65. Tommie Agee
66. Bobby Richardson (1960 Yankees)
67. Sandy Koufax (Los Angeles Dodgers)
68. Bob Gibson (Cardinals)
69. Reggie Jackson (1973 Oakland A's and 1977 Yankees)
70. Larry Sherry (Los Angeles Dodgers)
71. Joe McCarthy (1929)
72. Frank Chance (1907–8)
73. Bill Terry (1936–37)
74. Billy Southworth (1942–44 Cardinals and 1948 Boston Braves)
75. Charlie Dressen (1952–53)
76. Walter Alston (1955–56 Brooklyn Dodgers and 1965–66 Los Angeles Dodgers)

77. Sparky Anderson (1975–76 Reds and 1984 Tigers)
78. Hughie Jennings (1907–9 Tigers)
79. Joe McCarthy (1936–39 Yankees)
80. Casey Stengel (1949–53 Yankees)
81. Ralph Houk (1961–62 Yankees)
82. Dick Williams
83. Tony La Russa (1988–90 Oakland A's; 1996–97 Cardinals)
84. Frankie Frisch (1934 Cardinals)
85. Gabby Hartnett (1938 Cubs)
86. Tracy Stallard (Red Sox)
87. Ed Barrow (1918)
88. Luke Sewell (1944); Tommy and Joe, the Hall of Famer)
89. Burt Shotton (1947 and 1949 Brooklyn Dodgers)
90. Dallas Green (1980)
91. Harry Heilmann (1921, 1923, 1925, and 1927 Tigers)
92. Clarence Rowland (1917)
93. Bob Lemon (1948 Indians)
94. Willie Stargell (1979 Pirates; he shared the award with Keith Hernandez of the Cardinals.)
95. Roy Face (Pirates)
96. Bob Friend (Pirates)
97. Paul Molitor (1994 Blue Jays)
98. Ted Williams (Red Sox)
99. Rogers Hornsby (Cardinals)
100. Ted Williams (Red Sox)

Chapter Three Score

Number of Hits (Correct Answers) _____

Number of At Bats (Questions) _____

Season Batting Average _____

Twinkletoes

The 1936 Yankees had a record five players deliver 100 or more runs: Lou Gehrig (152), Joe DiMaggio (125), Tony Lazzeri (109), Bill Dickey (107), and the right fielder who succeeded Babe Ruth (107).

Ruth's replacement was a pretty good ballplayer. He batted .290 with 108 home runs over nine seasons. During that period he helped the Yankees to five world titles in six tries. Besides 1936, he had a banner year in 1939, when he batted .306, belted a career-high 21 home runs, and drove home 101 runs.

Who was "Twinkletoes"?

BONUS QUESTION #8
Rapid Rise

It is hard to fathom that a 17-year-old pitcher could break into the major leagues in the following fashion:

On August 23, 1936, this right-hander struck out 15 batters in his first major-league start, which was only two strikeouts shy of Dizzy Dean's big-league mark.

On September 13, he proceeded to strike out 17 Philadelphia Athletics batters to set an American League record and tie Dean's major-league mark.

Then, after a 5–3 season of 62 innings, he went home to Van Meter, Iowa, to graduate from high school.

Name this young phenom.

Hammerin' Hank

Hank Greenberg captivated the imagination of the American public in 1938 when he was within two home runs of Babe Ruth's cherished mark of 60 with five games left in the season.

"Hammerin' Hank" went homerless in his next three games. On the final day of the season, he had a double-header against the Indians to make up the difference.

Greenberg had a good afternoon, connecting for four hits in eight official at bats. But the Cleveland pitchers kept his hits in the park.

He got three singles in the second game. In the first game he was held to one safety by a 19-year-old pitcher who struck out a record 18 batters in one game.

Ironically, that young phenom, on the most celebrated afternoon of his young career, lost the game, 4–1.

Who is he?

Chapter Four

Casey, Jimmy, and the Kid

1. Who led his league in ERA an American League—record four consecutive years? (He won 300 career games for two American League clubs.)
2. Whose five opening-game Fall Classic wins is a World Series record? (Six out of seven times this eight-time .300 hitter played on the world championship club.)
3. Name the pitcher who in 1949 became the first hurler to lead his league in ERA (2.50) with a losing (11–14) record. (He defeated Allie Reynolds of the Yankees in game one of the 1951 World Series.)
4. Identify the only player to win Rookie of the Year (1949), Most Valuable Player (1956), and

the Cy Young Award (1956). (He was winless in four World Series decisions.)

5. Who was the last Yankee to win Rookie of the Year? (He also pitched a no-hitter.)

6. Which first baseman was the first one to win back-to-back MVP awards? (He won back-to-back home run titles, too.)

7. Name the only second baseman to win consecutive MVP awards. (His team won back-to-back world titles in the same years.)

8. Who was the only player to twice steal three bases in a World Series game? (In 1974, he stole a National League–record 118 bases in one season.)

9. Name the only third baseman to win consecutive MVP awards. (He won back-to-back home run titles, too.)

10. Identify the only catcher to cop consecutive MVP awards. (Though he hit 358 lifetime homers, he never won a four-base title.)

11. Who was the first of two outfielders in the National League to win back-to-back MVP titles? (He also won consecutive home run titles.)

12. Who hit a record nine home runs in three consecutive World Series? (He hit .625 in the 1927 World Series, the second all-time high.)

13. Name the only right fielder to win back-to-back MVP honors. (He won the RBI title in both years also.)

14. Identify the only center fielder to cop consecutive MVP awards. (He won the Triple Crown in the first of those two years.)

15. Another, more recent, first baseman won back-to-back MVP titles. (He put the "Big Hurt" on contemporary American League pitchers.) Who is he?

16. What World War II pitcher has been the only moundsman to win consecutive MVP honors? (He led the league in wins from 1944 to 1946.)

17. Who was the manager who won a record 10 pennants but closed out his checkered career with four straight tenth-place finishes? (In fact, he ended up in the second division in each of his first nine years, all in the National League.)

18. Which Hall of Famer pitched a shutout in each of three consecutive (1906–8) World Series? (He had only three fingers on his pitching hand.)

19. Who was the Hall of Fame pitcher who toiled 21 years in the majors without ever striking out 100 batters in a season? (He did complete 74 percent of the games he started, though.)

20. Which National League power hitter connected for 40 or more home runs in each season from 1953 to 1957? (He won only one home run title.)

21. Name the all-round player who averaged 50 home runs a season in the four years he won four-base titles. (Twice he hit more than 50 home runs in a season.)

22. Which Hall of Famer scored more than 100 runs in 13 consecutive seasons and knocked home more than 100 runs in 13 consecutive years? (He played on six consecutive world title teams.)

23. Which .330 lifetime batter hit .300 with four dif-

ferent teams? (He won a batting title with the 1926 Tigers.)

24. Name the .334 lifetime hitter who batted .300 for four different teams. (He won back-to-back batting titles.)

25. What Hall of Famer was traded by the New York Giants to the Cardinals for Hall of Famer Rogers Hornsby? (He said that his 16-year career passed in a "flash.")

26. Identify the third baseman, a .306 lifetime hitter, who batted .300 or better for eight straight years (1946–53) in the American League. (He won the batting crown in 1949.)

27. Who hit 361 lifetime homers and averaged only one strikeout per four-base blow? (He averaged only 28 strikeouts per season.)

28. Name the only second baseman to hit 300 (301) home runs in his career. (He once hit 42 and twice hit 39 home runs in a season.)

29. Two pitchers have won the Cy Young Award four times. Who was the left-hander? (He won 329 career games.)

30. Who is the right-hander? (He won it a record four consecutive years.)

31. The first relief pitcher to win the Cy Young Award was who? (He appeared in a record 106 games and set league highs that year in wins, with 15, and losses, with 12.)

32. Who was the first relief pitcher in the American League to win the Cy Young Award? (After Goose Gossage joined the club, he went from

Cy to *Sayonara*, according to teammate Graig Nettles.)

33. Identify the last Yankees pitcher to win the Cy Young Award. (Twice he led the American League in wins.)

34. Which 20-year-old player led the American League in batting in his second full season? (Though he was a .297 lifetime hitter, he never batted close to .340 again.)

35. Which 39-year-old player won the batting title with a .388 average? (The following year, he set a record when he became the only 40-year-old player to win the batting title.)

36. Which 29-year-old New York Giants rookie (1952) ended up pitching for 21 years? (He pitched in a record 1,070 games.)

37. Which 42-year-old pitcher led his league in saves in his final season? (As a 34-year-old rookie with Bill McKechnie's Boston Braves in 1937, he won 20 games.)

38. Which one of the following pitchers was a Cy Young Award winner: Jim Lonborg, Robin Roberts, Jim Bunning, or Jim Kaat?

39. Which 40-year-old player stole 25 bases? (Careerwise, this veteran of four World Series—1974, 1977–78, and 1981—stole 557 bases.)

40. Whose seven consecutive hits in the 1990 World Series is a record? (He also hit a record .750 in that Fall Classic.)

41. Who struck out only four times in 524 official at bats in his final season? (Careerwise, he

struck out an average of only eight times a
season.)

42. Which .312 lifetime hitter led the American
    League in safe pinch hits in his last three years
    in the majors? (He won one batting title and
    four home run crowns.)

43. Two hurlers pitched 20-year careers with the
    White Sox. (The first one won 254 games and
    an additional 3 in the 1917 World Series.) Who
    was he?

44. The second one won 260 games and twice led
    his league with wins. (He never played on a
    pennant-winning team. In fact, he rarely per-
    formed for a first-division club.) Who was he?

45. Whose 18 years with the Yankees was the lon-
    gest tenure of any pinstripe player? (He played
    in 12 World Series and hit a record 18 home
    runs in the Fall Classic.)

46. Identify the National League player who had
    only one manager during his 14-year career.
    (He, like his mentor, managed a World Series
    winner.)

47. Who was the record .439 hitter in four World
    Series who went on to become the president of
    the American League? (He also became a fa-
    mous cardiologist.)

48. Name the .286 lifetime hitter with 202 career
    home runs who went on to become the presi-
    dent of the National League. (From 1962 to 1964,
    he batted .300 each year and drove home 100
    runs in each season.)

49. Which catcher for five teams, over a 15-year ca-

reer, later became a secret agent for the United States government during World War II? (Lifetime, he batted .243 and hit six home runs.)

50. Whose number (44) was retired by a team in each league? (Three times he won home run crowns with that number.)

51. Name the manager whose number (37) was retired by a team in each league. (The number of full years he played and managed adds up to 37, too.)

52. The numbers of three playing managers have been retired. Who wore number 4 for the Red Sox? (He won two pennants, one with each of two different teams, and he batted .301 lifetime.)

53. Who wore number 5 for the Indians? (He won one batting crown and one world title.)

54. Who wore number 4 for the New York Giants? (Lifetime, he batted .304 and hit 511 homers.)

55. The Angels retired the number (26) of a man who never played or managed in the majors. (He had a horse named Champion, though.) Who is he?

56. A Yankees and Tigers right fielder wore at various times during his career three numbers that were ultimately retired: Babe Ruth's 3, Mickey Mantle's 7, and Hank Greenberg's 5. Who is he?

57. In 10 seasons he batted .300 nine times and .322 lifetime. (He played in four consecutive World Series, 1921 to 1924, for John McGraw's New York Giants. At 30, he died of Bright's disease.) Who was he?

58. What Reds catcher took his own life during Cin-

cinnati's pennant-winning season of 1940? (In three years as a part-time player, he batted .316.)

59. Name the Pirates pitcher who died during an emergency appendectomy operation in 1949. (He was 21–5 for the 1942 Yankees. His son Bill also pitched in the majors.)

60. Who was the perfect-game pitcher who died at the age of 31? (He had a career ERA of 1.88, the second-best all-time mark in that category.)

61. Which Cubs second baseman was killed in a 1964 airplane crash? (He won Rookie of the Year in 1962.)

62. Which batting champ with the 1903 Senators fell to his death from a bridge near Niagara Falls? (He twice hit .400 in the 1890s and batted .345 over a 16-year career.)

63. Name the .317 hitter over 18 seasons who died in a plane crash after the 1972 season, en route to an event supporting a humanitarian cause. (He won four batting titles.)

64. Who pitched in the majors at the record-low age of 15? (He didn't win his first game until he was 24. Overall, he was 135–117.)

65. Which shortstop was the youngest regular player in American League history? (He ended his career with more than 3,000 hits.)

66. Which Orioles pitcher won the most single-season games (19) as a teenager? (He pitched a 1–0 shutout in the 1966 World Series.)

67. Which New York Giant hit for the highest single-season average (.322) as a teenager? (He won six home run titles.)

68. Who hit the most single-season home runs (24) as a teenager? (The following year, at 20, he won the home run title.)

69. Who was the teenager who pitched five shut-outs in one year? (At 19, he was a rookie for the 1967 Reds.)

70. Name the first black player to homer in his first at bat. (A pitcher, he never hit another one. But he was the first black pitcher to appear in a World Series—as a pinch runner.)

71. Who was the famous relief pitcher who hit a home run in his first at bat? (Over 21 years he never hit another one.)

72. Who was the highly successful manager who got four hits in his first major-league game? (In the 1923 World Series he hit two game-winning home runs for the New York Giants.)

73. Name the 1959 Rookie of the Year and the 1969 MVP who got four hits, including two triples, in his first game. (He's known more for homers than triples, though.)

74. Who was the only rookie to win a batting title? (He won one the following year also.)

75. Which pitcher, in a strike-abbreviated season, tied a rookie record when he hurled eight shut-outs? (He won both Rookie of the Year and the Cy Young Award that season.)

76. Who got a rookie-record 223 hits? (He and his brother are both in the Hall of Fame.)

77. Name the Cardinal infielder whose home run won the 1950 All-Star Game for the National

League. (He played on world title teams with two different clubs.)

78. What rookie pitcher won three games in the 1909 World Series? (Sixteen years later he pitched in his next World Series, with the same team.)

79. Name the pitcher who, in five full seasons with the Cardinals, averaged 24 victories a season. (He pitched in the Fall Classic with the winning Redbirds and the losing Cubs.)

80. What 1961 team lost a record 23 consecutive games? (Gene Mauch was the manager.)

81. Name the 1973 club that won the National League pennant with the lowest (.508) winning percentage. (Managed by Yogi Berra, they extended the Oakland A's to seven games before losing in the World Series.)

82. A 1916 club won a record 26 consecutive games. (It finished in fourth place.) What team was it?

83. Who shares the modern major-league record for most runs scored (9) in two consecutive games? (He was a rookie at the time.)

84. What 1906 team won a record 116 games for a record .763 winning percentage? (Frank Chance was its manager.)

85. Name the 1935 club that won a record 21 consecutive games without a tie. (The 1916 New York Giants won 26 consecutive games but had one tie contest in their streak.)

86. Identify the person who played in the World Series with a record four different teams, includ-

ing the 1991–92 Atlanta Braves, with whom he hit four home runs.

87. Name the last manager of the Browns. (As a player, he got into the World Series four times within five years. A shortstop, he was the glue of his team's infield.)

88. Identify the last skipper (1967) of the Kansas City Athletics. (He retired from the position of shortstop after 20 years, with a .310 lifetime average.)

89. Who was the first manager (1961) of the Twins? (He once got the only hit for the Brooklyn Dodgers in a World Series game.)

90. Who was the first manager (1972) of the Rangers? (He led the American League in RBIs six straight times.)

91. Name the third baseman in the 1951 Senators infield of Mickey Vernon, Cass Michaels, and Pete Runnels. (He led the league in walks six times.)

92. Pinpoint the third baseman in the 1964 Cardinals infield of Bill White, Julian Javier, and Dick Groat. (He won MVP in 1964, the year he hit a grand slam in the World Series.)

93. Who was the third baseman in the 1974 Oakland A's infield of Gene Tenace, Dick Green, and Bert Campaneris? (His son Chris played for the Indians.)

94. The Meusel brothers played left field for opposing New York teams in the 1921–23 World Series. Who was the .309 lifetime hitter who

played for the Yankees? (He won the home run title in 1925.)

95. Who was the .310 lifetime hitter who played for the New York Giants? (From 1922 to 1925 he drove home better than 100 runs in each season.)

96. Only one pair of brothers ever won batting titles. (Which one of them won it with the 1944 Brooklyn Dodgers?)

97. Which one of them copped it with the 1947 Cardinals and Phillies?

98. Two brothers won Cy Young awards. Which of them did it twice?

99. Which of them did it once? (He did it with the 1970 Twins.)

100. What manager guided a record four different teams in the Championship Series? (He won back-to-back pennants with one of them.)

Chapter Four Answers

1. Bob "Lefty" Grove (1929–32 Philadelphia Athletics: Athletics and Red Sox)
2. Red Ruffing (Yankees)
3. Dave Koslo (New York Giants)
4. Don Newcombe (Brooklyn Dodgers)
5. Dave Righetti (1981 and 1983)
6. Jimmie Foxx (1932–33 Philadelphia Athletics)
7. Joe Morgan (1975–76 Reds)
8. Lou Brock (1967–68 Cardinals)
9. Mike Schmidt (1980–81 Phillies; 1974–76, 1980–81 and 1983–84 Phillies)
10. Yogi Berra (1954–55 Yankees)
11. Dale Murphy (1982–83 and 1984–85 Atlanta Braves)
12. Babe Ruth (1926–28 Yankees)
13. Roger Maris (1960–61 Yankees)
14. Mickey Mantle (1956–57 Yankees)
15. Frank Thomas (1993–94 White Sox)
16. Hal Newhouser (1944–45 Tigers)
17. Casey Stengel (1949–60 Yankees and 1962–65 Mets)
18. Mordecai Brown (Cubs)

19. Ted Lyons (White Sox)
20. Duke Snider (1956 Brooklyn Dodgers)
21. Willie Mays (1955 New York Giants; 1962, 1964–65 San Francisco Giants)
22. Lou Gehrig (1926–38 Yankees)
23. Heinie Manush (Tigers, Browns, Senators, and Brooklyn Dodgers)
24. Al Simmons (Philadelphia Athletics, White Sox, Tigers, and Senators; 1930–31 Athletics)
25. Frankie Frisch
26. George Kell (Tigers and Red Sox)
27. Joe DiMaggio (Yankees)
28. Rogers Hornsby (1922 Cardinals; 1925 Cardinals and 1929 Cubs)
29. Steve Carlton (1972, 1977, 1980, and 1982 Phillies)
30. Greg Maddux (1992–95 Atlanta Braves)
31. Mike Marshall (1974 Los Angeles Dodgers)
32. Sparky Lyle (1977 Yankees)
33. Ron Guidry (1978; 1978 and 1985)
34. Al Kaline (1955 Tigers)
35. Ted Williams (1957–58 Red Sox)
36. Hoyt Wilhelm
37. Jim Turner (1945 Yankees)
38. Jim Lonborg (1967 Red Sox)
39. Davey Lopes (1986 Cubs and Astros)
40. Billy Hatcher (Reds)
41. Joe Sewell (1933 Yankees)
42. Johnny Mize (1951–53 Yankees)
43. Red Faber
44. Ted Lyons
45. Mickey Mantle (1951–68 Yankees)

46. Gil Hodges (Walter Alston; 1969 Mets)
47. Bobby Brown (1947, 1949, 1950–51 Yankees)
48. Bill White (Cardinals)
49. Moe Berg
50. Hank Aaron (Braves and Brewers)
51. Casey Stengel (Yankees and Mets)
52. Joe Cronin (1933 Senators and 1946 Red Sox)
53. Lou Boudreau (1944 and 1948)
54. Mel Ott
55. Gene Autry
56. Cliff Mapes
57. Ross Youngs
58. Willard Hershberger
59. Ernie Bonham
60. Addie Joss (1902–10 Indians)
61. Kenny Hubbs
62. Ed Delahanty
63. Roberto Clemente (1961, 1964–65, and 1967 Pirates)
64. Joe Nuxhall (1944 Reds)
65. Robin Yount (18 for the 1974 Brewers)
66. Wally Bunker (He was 19 in 1964.)
67. Mel Ott (He was 19 in 1928.)
68. Tony Conigliaro (1964 Red Sox)
69. Gary Nolan
70. Dan Bankhead (1947 Brooklyn Dodgers)
71. Hoyt Wilhelm (1952 New York Giants)
72. Casey Stengel (1912 Brooklyn Dodgers)
73. Willie McCovey (San Francisco Giants)
74. Tony Oliva (1964–65 Twins)
75. Fernando Valenzuela (1981 Los Angeles Dodgers)
76. Lloyd Waner (1927 Pirates; Paul)

77. Red Schoendienst (1946 Cardinals and 1957 Milwaukee Braves)
78. Babe Adams (Pirates)
79. Dizzy Dean (1932–36; 1934 and 1938)
80. Phillies
81. Mets
82. New York Giants
83. Mark McGwire (1987 A's)
84. Cubs
85. Cubs
86. Lonnie Smith (1980 Phillies, 1982 Cardinals, and 1985 Royals)
87. Marty Marion (1942–44 and 1946 Cardinals)
88. Luke Appling
89. Harry "Cookie" Lavagetto
90. Ted Williams (1941–42 and, after time out for military service, 1946–49 Red Sox)
91. Eddie Yost
92. Ken Boyer
93. Sal Bando
94. Bob
95. Emil
96. Fred "Dixie" Walker
97. Harry Walker
98. Gaylord Perry (1972 Indians and 1978 Padres)
99. Jim Perry
100. Billy Martin (1970 Twins, 1972 Tigers, the winning 1976–77 Yankees, and 1981 Oakland A's)

Chapter Four Score

Number of Hits (Correct Answers)   _____

Number of At Bats (Questions)   _____

Season Batting Average   _____

BONUS QUESTION #10
The Dutch Master

In 1938, Reds manager Bill McKechnie developed another young pitcher, Johnny Vander Meer, the "Dutch Master," into a nationally acclaimed moundsman.

On June 11, the 23-year-old left-hander pitched a 3–0 no-hit victory over the Boston Bees.

Four days later, he pitched against the Dodgers in the first night game ever played at Ebbets Field, and although he walked eight Brooklyn batters, he hurled a record second consecutive no-hitter.

With one out in the ninth inning, he walked three consecutive batters, but after McKechnie walked out to the mound to calm him down, he got Ernie Koy to ground into a force-out and the playing manager to hit a fly ball out that ended the 6–3 Cincinnati win.

Who was that Dodgers shortstop, with the .247 lifetime and .219 season average, who should have sent up a pinch hitter in that spot? He played on two-of-two World Series winners, the 1928 Yankees and the 1934 Cardinals.

BONUS QUESTION #11
Twenty-Twenty

Three times he won 20 games in a season, for the 1938–40 Browns and Tigers. But also three times he lost 20 games in a campaign, for the Browns, Tigers, and Philadelphia Athletics. Overall, in a 20-year career, he won 211 games and lost 222.

Perhaps the crowning moment in his career came in 1940, when he was 21–5 with the pennant-winning Tigers. In that year's World Series, against the winning Reds, he won the opening game, 7–2, with his father watching in the stands. The following day his father died of a heart attack.

But four days later the Tigers twirler rebounded to shut out the Reds on three hits, 8–0. Two days after that, he was called upon to pitch the seventh game. For six innings he was up to the challenge, commanding a slim 1–0 lead, but in the seventh frame two doubles, a questionable decision on the part of a Bengals infielder, and a long fly decided the game and the Series in Cincinnati's favor, 2–1.

Can you name that pitcher who has been the only major-league hurler to post a losing record with 200 or more wins and losses?

Baseball's Best Wartime Team

The 1942–44 St. Louis Cardinals, under the leadership of manager Billy Southworth, became the first National League team since John McGraw's 1921–24 New York Giants to win as many as three pennants in a row. In World Series play during that time, they defeated the Yankees in five games, lost to the Bombers in five contests, and outlasted the Browns in six games.

During that era, Cardinals players won the MVP award in three consecutive years: Mort Cooper in 1942, Stan Musial in 1943, and Marty Marion in 1944.

The Redbirds fielded a solid team against the Browns in the "Trolley Series" in 1944, especially since they had lost such standout players as Terry Moore, Enos Slaughter, and Harry Walker to the military service.

The starting lineup had three .300 hitters: Stan Musial (.347), Johnny Hopp (.336), and Walker Cooper (.317). Ray Sanders hit 12 home runs and paced the Cardinals with 102 RBIs. Whitey Kurowski smacked 20 four-base blows and delivered 87 runs.

Mort Cooper led the pitchers with 22 wins. Left-hander Max Lanier and a right-hander each won 17 contests. Harry Brecheen copped 16 victories, and George Munger added 11.

Munger was inducted into the service in July. But the Redbirds got an unexpected break when one of their pitchers was released from the service because he developed a stomach ulcer.

Who was that right-hander who went on to post a 17–4 record with the 1944 Cardinals? Four years later, he led the league in wins (10) and saves (9) out of the bull pen. In 1951, with the Cardinals and the Pirates, he again led the league in saves, with 13.

Chapter Five

Dizzy, Ernie, and the Man

1. Two brothers won two games apiece for a team that won a World Series. Which of them is in the Hall of Fame? (He led the National League in strikeouts from 1932 to 1935.)
2. Which of them isn't, but won 19 games in each of his first two seasons?
3. Two brothers, playing in the same outfield, got 200 or more hits many times. (Both of them are in the Hall of Fame.) Which of them did it eight times?
4. Which of them did it four times?
5. Identify the native American who started the opening game of three consecutive World Series. (He and Bob Feller used to team up by pitching opposite ends of a doubleheader for the Indians.)

6. Name the "Chief" who hit a single-season-high .358 for catchers in the National League. (He played for John McGraw's New York Giants at the time.)

7. Who was the hero of the 1912 Olympics who later batted .252 over a six-year career? (In 1919 he broke up baseball's only double no-hit nine-inning game with a single in the tenth inning that drove home the only run in the Reds' 1–0 victory over the Cubs.)

8. What native American player once hit a record 18 home runs in one month? (He won the American League home run crown in 1943.)

9. Identify the 15-year pitcher with a standoff 92–92 record whose name is Calvin Coolidge Julius Caesar Tuskhoma———? (His nickname is Buster.)

10. One pitcher was known as his team's "Meal Ticket." (He won more than 20 games a season every year from 1933 to 1937.) Who was he?

11. National League teams, especially the Brooklyn Dodgers, stood in awe of the "Man." Who was this seven-time batting-title winner?

12. He hit only 96 career four-base blasts, but they called him Home Run. Who was the four-time home run champ?

13. Who was called the Staten Island Scot? (He once hit a pennant-winning home run.)

14. Name the 1945 batting titlist whose nickname was Snuffy. (He died in a train accident.)

15. What manager won a record five Championship Series? (He won at least one in each league.)

16. He played and coached in a record 23 World

Series. (That's certainly something to "Crow" about.) Who is he?

17. Who was the first Heisman Trophy winner to play in the majors? (He won the honor with the 1950 Ohio State Buckeyes.)

18. Who was the first man to play in both a Rose Bowl and a World Series? (He won the MVP award in 1958.)

19. Name the only college All-American basketball player to win the MVP award. (He played for Duke and the Pirates.)

20. Who was a 21-game winner for the 1936 White Sox who was also the winner of the decathlon at the Penn Relays in 1927? (He won 104 lifetime games with seven teams.)

21. Who was the 1979 pitcher who led the National League in both wins (21) and losses (20)? Though he pitched in the major leagues for 24 years, he never played in the World Series.

22. Who played in a National League-record 1,207 consecutive games? (He batted .294 and hit 272 home runs in 19 years.)

23. Whose previous record did he break? (The outfielder played in 1,117 consecutive games. He batted .290 and hit 426 career homers.)

24. Which pitcher, with 273 regular-season wins, was missing a couple of toes on his pivot foot? (He won seven of nine World Series contests.)

25. Name the first player with glasses to win a batting title. (He did it with the 1931 Cardinals.)

26. Identify the outfielder with one arm who played one season with the 1945 Browns. (He batted .218.)

27. Who was the first catcher to wear glasses? (They called him Scrap Iron.)

28. Identify the former Yankees pitcher who umpired in a Fall Classic. (He was 3–0 in World Series play.)

29. Name the first umpire to wear glasses. (As a pitcher, he won 171 games, all with the Philadelphia Athletics.)

30. Who was the onetime three-game winner in a Fall Classic who also umpired in a World Series? (He won those three games for the first world champs, the 1903 Red Sox.)

31. What player won two of two decisions for the Cubs in Fall Classic play and later umpired in a World Series? (He pitched in the 1932 and 1935 World Series.)

32. Who was the owner of the Brooklyn Dodgers when they moved to Los Angeles? (His son Peter replaced him as owner.)

33. Who was the owner of the Yankees when they first rose to prominence in the 1920s? (A beer baron, his dynasty lasted into the early 1940s.)

34. Name the owner and president of the 1948 World Series–winning Indians and the 1959 pennant-winning White Sox whose father was the owner of the flag-copping 1929 Cubs.

35. Who owned the White Sox during their scandal-plagued season of 1919? (He was called the Old Roman.)

36. Identify the native of Chartham, Ontario, Canada, whose 284 career wins are the most gar-

nered by a black pitcher. (Seven times he won 20 games in a season.)

37. Born in Ozanna, Poland, this player starred for the Orioles in the 1966 World Series. (In game one he struck out a record 11 men in relief.) What was his name?

38. A native of Glasgow, Scotland, he hit the "Shot Heard 'Round the World." (He hit 264 lifetime homers. Six times he hit more than 20 circuit clouts in a season for the New York Giants.) Who is he?

39. Name the first Latin-born player to become Rookie of the Year in the American League. (He won the stolen-base title for a major league–record nine consecutive years.)

40. Who was the first Latin-born player to win an MVP award? (He won it with the 1965 Twins.)

41. Name the first native of Puerto Rico to win 20 games in a season. (He was 0–2 in postseason play for the 1976–77 Yankees.)

42. What native of Cuba became the first Hispanic to win 20 games in a season? (He did it with the 1923 Reds.)

43. This native of the Dominican Republic twice led National League pitchers in wins. (Six times he won 20 games in a season.) Who is he?

44. Name the pitcher who in his last eight years in the majors won the first eight Gold Glove awards that were given at his position. (He won MVP with the 1952 Philadelphia Athletics.)

45. Who won the Gold Glove award for a record 16 consecutive seasons? (He won MVP in 1964.)

46. What pitcher won 14 consecutive Gold Glove awards? (He won 283 lifetime games.)

47. Lou Gehrig and what other first baseman finished their careers with a .340 lifetime average? (A Hall of Famer, he never played in a World Series.)

48. Two Yankees Hall of Fame outfielders finished their careers with .325 lifetime averages. Which one of them played with Babe Ruth?

49. Which one of them played with Mickey Mantle?

50. What 1988 pitcher struck out a record 20 batters in a seven-game Championship Series? (He once won Rookie of the Year (1984) and the Cy Young Award (1985) in back-to-back years.)

51. Who won 288 lifetime games, the most by any pitcher who did not win 300? (He once won 20 games with the Los Angeles Dodgers and twice won 20 games with the Yankees.)

52. Identify the pitcher who won 251 regular-season games and seven World Series contests. (He turned in a 1.12 ERA in 1968 and a 2.91 ERA lifetime.)

53. What pitcher was bought by the New York Giants for $11,000? (At first, he was called the $11,000 Lemon. Later, he hurled in World Series for the Giants and the Brooklyn Dodgers.)

54. Name the 1921 Reds pitcher who allowed just one home run in 301 innings of pitching, a National League record for the post–dead ball era. (He won 266 games for the Phillies and the Reds, and he completed 552 of 692 starts.)

55. Who, with the 1915–33 Senators, was Sam Rice's road roommate for a record 18 years? (A first baseman, he batted .298 lifetime.)

56. Name the 1935 Cubs outfielder who played an entire 154-game schedule without grounding into a double play. (A .300 hitter with the Cubs and Brooklyn Dodgers, he had 646 at bats.)

57. Whose uniform number was the first one to be retired? (He wore number 4.)

58. Which team was the first to wear plastic helmets? (It instituted the move after two of its promising young stars were beaned in 1941.)

59. What 1956 pitcher allowed a National League-record 46 home runs in one season? (He won 286 games.)

60. Who in 1970 tested the reserve clause in a controversial case? (When the Cardinals, for whom he played in three World Series, traded him to the Phillies, he refused to report to his new team.)

61. Which 1972 pitcher became the first hurler to win 200 career games without posting a 20-win season? (He was traded by the Orioles to the Reds for Frank Robinson.)

62. Name the present-day slugger who in 1990 set a major-league record when he struck out 10 times in three consecutive games.

63. Who was the first designated hitter? (He batted .293 lifetime for the Yankees and the White Sox.)

64. Name the 1982 San Francisco Giants pitcher who didn't allow a home run in a record 269⅓ innings over a period of four years. (From 1980 to 1984, he posted 111 saves.)

65. Which pitcher with 300 career wins took the longest time to reach that number? (A 321–game

lifetime winner, he posted only one 20-win season, with the 1976 Los Angeles Dodgers.)

66. What 1986 pitcher granted a record 50 home runs in one season? (He won five of six postseason games with the Pirates and the Twins.)

67. Name the Tigers pitcher who was known as the Yankee Killer in the 1950s and 1960s. (He won 21 games in 1956 and 23 in 1961.)

68. Name the present-day player who batted an American League–record .349 as a rookie in 1982.

69. Who got the last hit off Sandy Koufax? (He has managed the Mets, Reds, and Orioles.)

70. What shortstop holds the all-time single-season record for home runs at his position? (He won home run crowns in 1958 and 1960.)

71. Name the player who collected a record nine hits in an 18-inning contest. (An infielder, he batted .284 in nine seasons with the Indians and the Braves.)

72. Who pitched a record four consecutive winning complete games in Championship Series play? (He won three Cy Young Awards, in 1973, 1975, and 1976.)

73. Two players got a National League–record 254 hits in one season. (They did it in back-to-back years.) Who did it for the 1929 Phillies? (He batted .398.)

74. Who did it for the 1930 New York Giants? (At .401, he was the last National League player to bat .400.)

75. In 1959, Harvey Haddix of the Pirates pitched a perfect game for 12 innings. (He lost to the

Milwaukee Braves, however, on a double in the thirteenth inning by a player who hit 336 career homers.) Who got the only hit off Haddix that day, in the unlucky thirteenth inning?

76. Which batter received the most intentional bases on balls in one season? (He won the MVP Award that year.)

77. Which Hall of Famer wore the uniforms of all four New York teams—the New York Giants, the Brooklyn Dodgers, the Yankees, and the Mets? (Careerwise, he hit .284 during the regular season and .393 in three World Series.)

78. Name the American League shortstop who hit the most home runs (40) by a player at his position. (He hit 97 home runs for the 1969–71 Red Sox.)

79. Which Hall of Famer won four American League batting titles, hitting over .390 each time? (From 1919 to 1930, 12 consecutive years, he hit .300 with the Tigers and the Reds.)

80. Identify the last pitcher to post back-to-back 30-win seasons. (Before he went into World War I he averaged 30 wins a season over a four-year period of time.)

81. Name the only pitcher to hurl a no-hitter in his first start. (He pitched only one complete game.)

82. Which pitcher posted a record 16 shutouts in one year? (He hurled a National League–record 90 career shutouts.)

83. Who holds the modern National League record with 37 wins in one season? (He tossed 80 lifetime shutouts.)

84. Who was the only pitcher to lead the league in

losses (23) one year and wins (27) the next? (A 171-game winner, he led the American League in saves three times.)

85. Name the only Reds player, in addition to Pete Rose, to win two or more batting titles. (He was a .323 lifetime hitter.)

86. Name the only pitcher to allow four consecutive home runs. (He averaged 15 wins a season for the 1956–59 Tigers.)

87. What 1962 Kansas City A's pitcher didn't allow a free pass in a record 84⅓ consecutive innings? (Mickey Mantle once almost hit one of his pitches out of Yankee Stadium.)

88. Name the only pitcher to lead his league in ERA for five consecutive years. (They were his last five years in the majors.)

89. In addition to Bobby Cox, only one manager has led the Braves to more than one pennant. (In one of those years, he led his club to a world title over the Yankees.) Who was he?

90. Which pitcher won the most World Series games without a defeat? (He was 3–1 in All-Star Game play.)

91. Who was the only person to play for the Braves in Boston, Milwaukee, and Atlanta? (He won two home run crowns.)

92. Whose career fielding average of .996 is the best ever recorded by a first baseman who played in at least 1,000 games? (He batted .356 in five Championship Series and .319 in five World Series.)

93. Whose 0.96 ERA with the 1914 Red Sox was the all-time-record low in that department until Den-

nis Eckersley spun an 0.61 mark with the 1990 Oakland A's? (His 11-year ERA with the Red Sox and the Tigers was 2.77; his ERA in the 1915–16 World Series with the Red Sox was 1.00.)

94. Whose 1.04 ERA with the 1906 Cubs is the all-time National League low in that category? (He won 239 regular-season games and five of nine World Series decisions.)

95. Identify the second baseman who didn't make an error in a record 123 consecutive games. (He won the MVP award in 1984 and the home run crown in 1990.)

96. Name the player who hit 177 triples, a record for any player active since 1941. (He and Sam Crawford led a league in triples a record five times.)

97. Two catchers have claimed a title for most triples. Who was the 1966 winner in the National League? (He was Steve Carlton's favorite backstop.)

98. Who was the 1972 catcher in the American League? (He won the Rookie of the Year award that year.)

99. Though he never won more than 23 games in a season, he led his league in victories a record nine times. (He also led his circuit in 20-win seasons a National League–record 13 times.) Who is he?

100. Hal Newhouser and what other Tigers pitcher won a combined total of 56 games in 1944, the highest total for two pitchers on the same club since 1920? Newhouser won 29. Who won 27?

Chapter Five Answers

1. Dizzy Dean (1934 Cardinals)
2. Paul Dean (1934–35 Cardinals)
3. Paul Waner
4. Lloyd Waner
5. Allie Reynolds (1951–53 Yankees)
6. John "Chief" Meyers (1912 New York Giants)
7. Jim Thorpe (New York Giants, Reds, and Boston Braves)
8. Rudy York (1937 Tigers)
9. Cal McLish
10. Carl Hubbell (New York Giants)
11. Stan Musial (1943, 1946, 1948, 1950–52, and 1957 Cardinals)
12. Frank Baker (1911–14 Philadelphia Athletics)
13. Bobby Thomson (1951 New York Giants)
14. George Stirnweiss (Yankees)
15. George "Sparky" Anderson (1970, 1972, 1975–1976 Reds; 1984 Tigers)
16. Frank Crosetti (1932, 1936–39, 1941–43, 1947, 1949–53, 1955–58, and 1960–64 Yankees)
17. Vic Janowicz (1953–54 Pirates)

18. Jackie Jensen (1949 California Golden Bears and 1950 Yankees; Red Sox)
19. Dick Groat (1960)
20. Vern Kennedy
21. Phil Niekro (Atlanta Braves)
22. Steve Garvey (Los Angeles Dodgers and Padres)
23. Billy Williams (Cubs)
24. Red Ruffing (1924–47 Red Sox, Yankees, and White Sox)
25. Chick Hafey
26. Pete Gray
27. Clint Courtney (1951 Yankees)
28. George Pipgras (1944)
29. Ed Rommel
30. Bill Dinneen
31. Lon Warneke
32. Walter O'Malley
33. Jake Ruppert
34. Bill Veeck (William)
35. Charles Comiskey
36. Ferguson Jenkins (1967–72 Cubs and 1974 Rangers)
37. Moe Drabowsky
38. Bobby Thomson (1951 New York Giants)
39. Luis Aparicio (1956–64 White Sox and Orioles)
40. Zoilo Versalles
41. Ed Figueroa
42. Dolf Luque
43. Juan Marichal (1963 and 1968 San Francisco Giants)
44. Bobby Shantz (1957–64)
45. Brooks Robinson (1960–75 Orioles)

46. Jim Kaat (1962–75 Twins and White Sox)
47. George Sisler (1915–30 Browns, Senators, and Boston Braves)
48. Earle Combs (1924–34 Yankees)
49. Joe DiMaggio (1951 Yankees)
50. Dwight Gooden (Mets)
51. Tommy John (1977 and 1979–80)
52. Bob Gibson (1959–75 Cardinals)
53. Rube Marquard (1911–13 Giants; 1916 and 1920 Dodgers)
54. Eppa Rixey (1912–33)
55. Joe Judge
56. Augie Galan
57. Lou Gehrig (1939 Yankees)
58. Brooklyn Dodgers (Pete Reiser and Pee Wee Reese)
59. Robin Roberts (Phillies)
60. Curt Flood
61. Milt Pappas (1966)
62. Jay Buhner (Mariners)
63. Ron Blomberg
64. Greg Minton
65. Don Sutton (20 years)
66. Bert Blyleven
67. Frank Lary
68. Wade Boggs (Red Sox)
69. Davey Johnson (1966 World Series with the Orioles; 1996 Orioles)
70. Ernie Banks (47 with 1958 Cubs)
71. Johnny Burnett (1932)
72. Jim Palmer (1969, 1970, 1971, and 1973 Orioles)
73. Frank "Lefty" O'Doul

74. Bill Terry
75. Joe Adcock
76. Willie McCovey (45 with the 1969 San Francisco Giants)
77. Casey Stengel (1916 Dodgers and 1922–23 Giants)
78. Rico Petrocelli (1969 Red Sox)
79. Harry Heilmann (1921, 1923, 1925, and 1927 Tigers)
80. Grover Alexander (1915–17 Phillies)
81. Bobo Holloman (1953 Browns)
82. Grover Alexander (1916 Phillies)
83. Christy Mathewson (1908 New York Giants)
84. Ed Rommel (1921–22 Philadelphia Athletics)
85. Edd Roush (1917 and 1919)
86. Paul Foytack (1963 Los Angeles Angels)
87. Bill Fischer
88. Sandy Koufax (1962–66 Los Angeles Dodgers)
89. Fred Haney (1957–58)
90. Lefty Gomez (Yankees)
91. Eddie Mathews (1953 and 1959)
92. Steve Garvey (1969–87 Los Angeles Dodgers and Padres)
93. Dutch Leonard
94. Mordecai Brown
95. Ryne Sandberg
96. Stan Musial (Cardinals)
97. Tim McCarver (Cardinals)
98. Carlton Fisk (Red Sox)
99. Warren Spahn
100. Dizzy Trout

Chapter Five Score

Number of Hits (Correct Answers)   _____
Number of At Bats (Questions)   _____
Season Batting Average   _____

BONUS QUESTION #13
The Brat

Ewell "the Whip" Blackwell of the 1947 Reds posted league and career highs in three different categories: wins (22), complete games (23), and strikeouts (193).

During the 1947 season, he got the opportunity to duplicate the feat that his teammate, Johnny Vander Meer, had performed in 1938—pitch two consecutive no-hitters.

A winner of 16 consecutive games that season, he pitched a no-hitter in the middle of the string, against the Braves on June 18. In his next start he needed only two outs in the ninth inning to repeat the "Dutch Master's" treat. But the Dodgers second baseman squirted a ground ball through the legs of the six-foot-six right-hander's legs into center field.

Asked after the game what he was thinking about as he watched Blackwell's attempt to tie his record, Vander Meer said, "If Ewell did it, I wanted to be the first one out on the field to shake his hand."

By the way, who was the "Brat" who broke up Blackwell's record-tying attempt? He played on three pennant winners with three different teams from 1948 to 1951.

BONUS QUESTION #14
Tiny

Do you know whose wife received the first death benefits from the player pension fund?

Her husband won 66 games for the Yankees during the 1942–45 war years, including 21 games during the 1942 season, when he paced American League hurlers in winning percentage (.808), complete games (22), and shutouts (6).

From 1941 to 1943, he pitched in three consecutive World Series with the Yankees, winning one of three decisions.

He was 24–22 for the 1947–49 Pirates. On September 15, 1949, he died on the operating table during surgery to remove his inflamed appendix.

Who was that 103–72 lifetime pitcher whose widow received a "tiny" $90 a month pension for ten years? He had a son Bill, who won 75 games with the 1971–80 Cubs and Reds.

BONUS QUESTION #15
A Close Shave

In the spring of 1946, just after the war, baseball was challenged by Mexican millionaire Jorge Pascual and his four brothers, who created the Mexican League and began to lure away from the major leagues some of American's highest-priced players.

The New York Giants lost seven players to the Mexican League, including a pitcher who eventually went on to win 119 games and one World Series contest in the majors. The Cardinals lost their premier pitcher, Max Lanier, in addition to infielder Lou Klein and hurler Fred Martin. The Brooklyn Dodgers lost outfielder Luis Olmo and catcher Mickey Owen.

Commissioner A. B. "Happy" Chandler outlawed the Mexican League and vowed that any major-league players who jumped to it would be barred from organized ball for five years if they tried to return.

Players who went to Mexico soon found out that the Mexican League was a shaky ship foundering on high seas. After they returned to the States in August, Danny Gardella, a former Giants outfielder who had jumped to the Mexican League, took the matter of blacklisting to the courts. The owners, who knew that they were not on solid footing legally, soon issued amnesties to all of the renegade players. Some players, however, were banned for as many as three years.

Who was that Giants stray—he lost four years in the majors because of his defection—who in 1950 pitched 45 consecutive scoreless innings, which was 1⅓ fewer innings than the National League-record 46⅓ consecutive scoreless frames that former Giants star Carl Hubbell had thrown? He was the losing pitcher the day Don Larsen pitched his perfect game against the Brooklyn Dodgers in the 1956 World Series.

Chapter Six

Johnny, Reggie, and Big Klu

1. Name the pitcher who made a record 594 consecutive starting assignments without a relief appearance. (He saved a game in the 1969 World Series.)
2. What player pitched a record 16 opening-game starting assignments, 13 in the National League and three times in the American League? (He won the Cy Young Award three times.)
3. Identify the pitcher who hurled a record 188 consecutive complete games. (He did it for the 1901–6 Cardinals and Cubs.)
4. Who was the first big "Bonus Baby"? (The Tigers gave $52,000 to this University of Michigan student in 1941.)
5. Name the first and only player to lead his

league in RBIs his first full three seasons in the majors? (He led his league in home runs the first two years.)

6. Who had the highest slugging average (.557) for a player with a lifetime batting average below .300? (He won the Triple Crown.)

7. What pitcher was the last to start both ends of a doubleheader? (He lost both games against the 1973 Yankees.)

8. What city was the only one to produce two Triple Crown winners in the same season? (It was in 1933.)

9. Identify the only Yankee to win both Rookie of the Year and the MVP crown. (He played on back-to-back World Series winners.)

10. One 300-game winner pitched a record four one-hitters in one year. (He never hurled a no-hitter.) Who was he?

11. Who retired a record 41 consecutive batters over two games in 1972? (He chalked up double-figure wins for the 1973–77 San Francisco Giants.)

12. What pitcher won a record 24 consecutive games over a two-year time span? (In those two years he twice defeated the Yankees in the World Series.)

13. At the age of 42, he started 20 games and completed 20 contests. (In 21 years he never struck out 100 batters in a season.) Who was he?

14. A switch-hitter, he grounded into only 38 double plays in 4,553 at bats, a ratio of only one to every 138 at bats, the best in history. (He played

in three World Series with the Orioles.) Who is he?

15. Identify the only catcher to field 1.000 in a season of at least 100 games. (He played in the 1941–42 World Series with the Yankees, but he set that record with the 1946 Philadelphia Athletics.)

16. Who caught a record four no-hitters? (The last one was Charlie Robertson's perfect game in 1922.)

17. Name the only catcher since Ernie Lombardi to bat .300 five times. (Three years in a row, he batted .300 and drove home 100 runs.)

18. Name the catcher who won a record 10 Gold Gloves. (Three times he won the RBI crown.)

19. Identify the only player to hit pinch-hit home runs in three consecutive official at bats. (His father, Al, was a catcher with the Tigers and the Reds.)

20. Whose .333 batting average is the best pinch-hitting average for substitute swingers with at least 100 at bats? (He hit a two-run home run in Cincinnati's only victory over the Yankees in the 1961 World Series.)

21. Recall the only player to pitch with two teams and in two leagues during a season in which he won the Cy Young Award. (The Indians traded him to the Cubs.)

22. What 39-year-old player became the oldest pitcher in the American League to win the Cy Young Award? (He had his best years with the

Indians, but he turned in his "last hurrah" season with the 1959 White Sox.)

23. What was the last year when a World Series was played in just one park? (George McQuinn's two-run homer defeated Mort Cooper in game one, 2–1.)

24. Name the Boston Braves catcher who scored the only run of game one of the World Series in 1948 when Tommy Holmes singled him home. (On the preceding play, he had appeared to be picked off second on a time play from Bob Feller to shortstop Lou Boudreau. Johnny Sain outdueled Feller, 1–0.)

25. Who was the 1968 Tigers second baseman who set an American League record when he played more than 150 games without grounding into a double play? (But he batted only .249, two points higher than his lifetime average. He did hit 197 career homers, though.)

26. What center fielder became the first player to win a Gold Glove in each league? (He was the American League's Rookie of the Year in 1966.)

27. Name the player who hit 39 home runs on his home grounds one year. (He hit *only* 19 four-base blows on the road.)

28. Whose league record did Babe Ruth break when he hit 29 home runs with the 1919 Red Sox? (An outfielder, this player hit 16 home runs with the 1902 Philadelphia Athletics.)

29. Whose major-league record did Babe Ruth break when he hit 29 home runs with the 1919 Red Sox? (He twice won three circuit clout crowns

in a row, hitting a career-high 24 with the 1915 Phillies.)

30. Who was the first player to hit 30 home runs in a season in each league? (This first baseman was called Dr. Strangeglove.)

31. Who was the former first baseman and outfielder who wrote a confessional best seller, *You Coulda Made Us Proud, Joe?* (He averaged 26 home runs a season from 1963–66.).

32. What pitcher had a win-loss record on opening day of 6–0? (He four times won 20 games for the Indians and twice copped 20 contests for the Red Sox.)

33. Name the 1960 Rookie of the Year with the Los Angeles Dodgers who later (1968–70) averaged 45 home runs a season with an American League team. (He hit 382 lifetime homers.)

34. Which one of the following players hit .300 in three consecutive years, in three different cities: Orlando Cepeda, Bill Madlock, Darrell Evans, or Willie Montanez?

35. Identify the only pitcher to hit two grand slams in one game. (He drove home nine runs that day, a record for a moundsman.)

36. Name the National League player who hit the most home runs (47) in a four-base race without winning the home run crown. (At the age of 35, in his only World Series, he hit three home runs and drove home 10 runs.)

37. Which of the following teams was the only one to have four players on it hit 30 or more home runs in a season: 1927 Yankees, 1947 New York

Giants, 1961 Yankees, or 1977 Los Angeles Dodgers?

38. Two players who won home run titles never hit another four-bagger in the majors. Dave Brain of the 1907 Boston Braves was one of them. Who was the 1905 Red?

39. Who hit a record 51 inside-the-park home runs? (He won six triple titles. In 1914 he set an American League record with 26 three-base blows.)

40. What player hit the most career homers without ever leading his league in that category? (He did lead the league in doubles eight times and triples five times, though.)

41. Name the last player to hit two inside-the-park homers in one game. (An infielder, he batted .333 in each of the 1987 and 1991 World Series, and he hit a home run over the fence in each Classic.)

42. Who hit the most home runs (35) in his last season? (A two-time home run champ, he also drove home the most runs, 94, in his final year.)

43. Whose .993 career fielding percentage is the highest outfield mark for a player with at least 10 seasons? (He had 1.000 fielding percentage marks in 1979, 1981, 1985, and 1986.)

44. Whose 392 consecutive errorless games and 938 miscue-free chances are records for an outfielder? (He established the mark from the onset of his career with the 1990 Oakland A's and continued it with the 1991–94 San Francisco Giants.)

45. Name the only outfielder to handle more than

520 chances more than once. (A two-time batting champ in the National league, he did it four times.)

46. Two outfielders won a record 12 Gold Glove awards. (Both of them were National Leaguers.) Name the .302 lifetime hitter.

47. Name the .317 career hitter.

48. Whose 13 shutouts in one season are an American League record? (In two back-to-back seasons, he averaged 30 wins a year.)

49. Whose 11 shutouts in one season are a record by a left-hander? (He won both MVP and the Cy Young Award that year.)

50. Name the last player to win three straight home run titles. (He hit more than 500 career homers.)

51. Name the infielder who had a ball kicked out of his glove in a key play, an attempted tag at second base, of the 1951 World Series. (He won the MVP award the previous year.)

52. What pitcher hurled a record six consecutive shutouts? (He also beaned a National League–record 154 batters during his career.)

53. A 217-game winner, he copped just four victories in 1935, all of them shutouts, which tied for the league lead in that department. (Winless in three World Series decisions with the New York Giants and Brooklyn Dodgers, he was called Fat Freddie.) Who was he?

54. Name the Mets pitcher who lost a record four consecutive shutouts. (No other pitcher has ever been blanked more than two times in a row.)

55. Single out the 300-game winner who in 1933

broke the Yankees' record streak of 308 games without being shut out. (That year he posted the most season wins in the American League for the fourth time.)

56. The pitcher who won league ERA titles a record nine times, eight of them with numbers under 3.00, finished his career with a 3.06 mark. Name that hurler with a 1.75 ERA in three consecutive World Series.

57. Identify the pitcher who threw a record 38 1–0 shutout wins. (Overall, he was involved in a record 64 shutout games that ended in 1–0 scores. Careerwise, he pitched a record 110 blankings.)

58. Recall the first pitcher to chalk up 100 career saves. (He led the American League in saves five times and picked up three more in the 1924–25 World Series. As a starter, he won 94 games for the Senators and Tigers.)

59. Who was the first pitcher to collect 200 career saves? (He did it with the 1969 California Angels. Overall, he won a record 123 games in relief.)

60. Name the first pitcher to save 300 career games. (A 1982 Brewer at the time, he earlier saved a record six World Series contests, two each in the 1972–74 World Series.)

61. What pitcher came on in relief for Babe Ruth, who got ejected after arguing a ball-four call to Washington's leadoff batter, Ray Morgan, and got 27 consecutive outs without another Senator reaching base? (He won three of four decisions for the Red Sox in the 1915–16 World Series.)

62. In his last game he pitched 17 innings in relief, allowing 14 runs and 29 hits, including most of Johnny Burnett's record nine hits in one game, yet ended up winning his 171st and last game. (Manager Connie Mack brought only two able-bodied pitchers to Cleveland with him on that trip. When Lew Krausse got knocked out of the box, this pitcher was in the "barrel.") Name him.

63. Two pitchers have thrown over 400 innings in a season twice. One of them once hurled a record 464 frames and picked up 40 wins in one season. Who was this right-hander, who posted the all-time career-low 1.82 ERA?

64. The second one did it for the 1903–4 New York Giants, a team for whom he won 31 and 35 games, respectively. Who was that "Iron Man"?

65. Two pitchers since 1920 have thrown 300 or more innings in at least four consecutive seasons. The National League pitcher did it six times, from 1950 to 1955, years in which he won 20 games a season. Who is he?

66. The American League pitcher did it four consecutive times, from 1971 to 1974, years in which he won 20 games a season. Who was that knuckleball pitcher?

67. Name the pitcher who staggered and reeled to a 19–16 victory, his last in the majors, knowing that it would put him in third place on the all-time-wins list. (That day he beat the team with whom he had won a rookie-record 28 games in 1911.)

68. On the same day in 1985 that Tom Seaver won his 300th game, who became the first infielder since Eddie Collins to get his 3,000th hit? (He won seven batting titles.)

69. Another pitcher picked up his 300th career win in 1985. Name this 318-game winner, who got it with the Yankees on the last day of the season.

70. Identify the only player to hit 40 home runs and steal 40 bases in the same season. (He won the home run crown and the MVP award that year.)

71. Name the only shortstop in American League history to bat .300, hit 30 home runs, and drive home 100 runs in the same season. (He hit more than 20 homers in each of his first 10 seasons, another junior circuit mark for shortstops.)

72. Who became the first second baseman in history to bat .300, hit 20 or more home runs, collect 200 or more hits, and drive home 100 runs two years in a row? (He also was the first player to homer from both sides of the plate in the same inning.)

73. Who won a San Francisco Giants club-record 16 consecutive games? (In that year's World Series he started three games—each of them against the Yankees Ralph Terry—and won one of three decisions.)

74. Two players were hit with more than 225 pitches in their careers. The all-time National League leader got plunked 243 times and a single-season-mark 50 times. Name that 1963–74 infielder.

75. The other player got hit an American League

career-high 227 times and a single-season-high 35 times. Who is that 1979 MVP winner with the Angels?

76. Who is the pitcher whose 1–0 shutout gave the Atlanta Braves their first world title? (He won the Cy Young Award in 1991; he won 20 games in each of the 1991–93 seasons.)

77. Whose passed ball with two outs in the ninth inning of the fourth game of the 1941 World Series gave the Yankees a 3–1 game lead in the Fall Classic?

78. Name the player who hit a record five home runs in one World Series. (He also hit a record seven round-trippers in back-to-back Fall Classics.)

79. Name the only player with a .600 slugging average and winning percentage. (A player needs a minimum of 100 pitching decisions to qualify.)

80. Identify the player who led his league in stolen bases a record 10 times. (An outfielder, he batted .285 and stole 738 bases lifetime. In the 1925 World Series he batted .458 for the Pirates.)

81. Whose 35 thefts of home are the all-time high? (His 96 stolen bases in 1915 was the longtime single-season record.)

82. Who got caught stealing a record 307 times? (In World Series play he stole successfully a record-tying 14 times.)

83. Whose World Series mark did the above player tie? (He stole 743 regular-season bases and a record 14 World Series bags for the 1906–30 Philadelphia Athletics and White Sox.)

84. What third baseman didn't commit an error in

a National League-record 97 consecutive games? (A utility player at the time, he set the mark in the 1966–68 seasons.)

85. Which center fielder struck out a record seven consecutive times in a Championship Series? (He played on a world title team that year—and the next one too.)

86. Who in six American League Championship Series set records in home runs (9) and triples (4)? (He also got a record 18 long hits.)

87. Three rookies have led their leagues in home runs. Who edged Johnny Mize by one, 23–22, in 1946?

88. Who beat out Walt Dropo, also a rookie, by three, 37–34, in 1950?

89. Who nipped George Bell by two, 49–47, in 1987?

90. The oldest rookie in history was 43. Who was he? (At 43, he was 5–1 with seven saves for the 1962 Pirates.)

91. Who was the oldest (42) 20-game winner? (He copped the last of his 13 20-win seasons in 1963.)

92. Name the only 30-game winner to later lose 20 contests in a season. (He was the Cy Young Award winner in both 1968 and 1969.)

93. Two pitchers lost three games in a World Series. Which one was trying to lose them?

94. Which one was trying to win them? (He lost them to the Los Angeles Dodgers in 1981.)

95. Whose 200-hit seasons in his first three years are the American League all-time high? (He might have added to that mark if his streak hadn't

been interrupted by three years in the military service during World War II.)

96. Name the player who got a record seven consecutive hits in back-to-back games in the 1993 American League Championship Series. (He is fourth on the all-time stolen-base list.)

97. Two pitchers struck out a National League rookie-record 15 batters in one game. Who was the 1954 Brooklyn Dodgers left-hander? (He won both of his decisions by shutout that year. Two years later, he was out of the majors for good.)

98. What 1971 Astros right-hander also did it? (He went on to become the only National League right-hander to twice strike out 300 batters in a season.)

99. Only one National League pitcher twice struck out 18 batters in a game. (In his first eight years, he averaged 4½ wins a season; in his last six seasons he averaged 21½ victories a year.) Who is he?

100. Nolan Ryan struck out 300 or more batters in a season a record six times. He also struck out 200 or more batters a record 14 times. But he didn't strike out 200 or more batters for a record number of consecutive seasons. One pitcher struck out 200 or more batters for a record nine consecutive seasons. But he never fanned 300 batters in a year. Who was that 1968–76 pitcher?

Chapter Six Answers

1. Nolan Ryan (1974–93 Angels, Astros, and Rangers)
2. Tom Seaver (1971–86 Mets, Reds, and White Sox)
3. Jack Taylor
4. Dick Wakefield
5. Cecil Fielder (1990–92 Tigers)
6. Mickey Mantle (.298 with the 1951–68 Yankees; 1956)
7. Wilbur Wood (White Sox)
8. Philadelphia (Chuck Klein, Phillies; Jimmie Foxx, Philadelphia Athletics)
9. Thurman Munson (1970 and 1976; 1977–78)
10. Grover Alexander (1915 Phillies)
11. Jim Barr
12. Carl Hubbell (1936–37 New York Giants)
13. Ted Lyons (1942 White Sox)
14. Don Buford (1963–72 Orioles)
15. Buddy Rosar
16. Ray Schalk (White Sox)
17. Thurman Munson (1970, 1973, 1975–77 Yankees)
18. Johnny Bench (1967–83 Reds)

19. Del Unser (1979 Phillies)
20. Gordy Coleman
21. Rick Sutcliffe (1984)
22. Early Wynn
23. 1944 (the Cardinals defeated the Browns at Sportsman's Park in St. Louis)
24. Phil Masi
25. Dick McAuliffe
26. Tommie Agee (1966 White Sox and 1970 Mets)
27. Hank Greenberg (1938 Tigers)
28. Ralph "Socks" Seybold
29. Gavvy Cravath
30. Dick Stuart (1961 Pirates, 1963 Red Sox)
31. Joe Pepitone (Yankees)
32. Wes Ferrell
33. Frank Howard (Senators)
34. Willie Montanez (1974–76 Phillies, San Francisco Giants, and Atlanta Braves)
35. Tony Cloninger (1966 Atlanta Braves)
36. Ted Kluszewski (1955 Reds and 1959 White Sox)
37. 1977 Dodgers: Steve Garvey, 33; Reggie Smith, 32; Ron Cey, 30; and Dusty Baker, 30)
38. Fred Odwell
39. Sam Crawford (Reds and Tigers)
40. Stan Musial (475)
41. Greg Gagne
42. Dave Kingman (1986 Oakland A's, 1979 Cubs and 1982 Mets)
43. Terry Puhl (Astros)
44. Darren Lewis
45. Richie Ashburn (Phillies)

46. Willie Mays (New York and San Francisco Giants)
47. Roberto Clemente (Pirates)
48. Jack Coombs (1910–11 Philadelphia Athletics)
49. Sandy Koufax (1963 Los Angeles Dodgers)
50. Mike Schmidt (1974–76 Phillies; 548)
51. Phil Rizzuto (Yankees; Eddie Stanky, New York Giants)
52. Don Drysdale (1968 Los Angeles Dodgers)
53. Freddie Fitzsimmons (New York Giants)
54. Jim McAndrew (Mets)
55. Lefty Grove (Philadelphia Athletics)
56. Lefty Grove (1929–31 Philadelphia Athletics)
57. Walter Johnson (1907–27 Senators)
58. Firpo Marberry
59. Hoyt Wilhelm (he played with nine teams)
60. Rollie Fingers (Oakland A's)
61. Ernie Shore
62. Eddie Rommel
63. Ed Walsh
64. Joe McGinnity
65. Robin Roberts (Phillies)
66. Wilbur Wood (White Sox)
67. Grover Alexander (he won the game with the Cardinals and defeated the Phillies)
68. Rod Carew (1985 Angels; August 4)
69. Phil Niekro
70. Jose Canseco (1988 Oakland A's)
71. Cal Ripkin (1991 Orioles; 1982–91 Orioles)
72. Carlos Baerga (Indians)
73. Jack Sanford (1962)
74. Ron Hunt

75. Don Baylor (he set the single-season mark with the 1986 Red Sox)
76. Tom Glavine (1995)
77. Mickey Owen (Brooklyn Dodgers)
78. Reggie Jackson (1977–78 Yankees)
79. Babe Ruth (.690 and .671 with the Red Sox, the Yankees, and the Boston Braves)
80. Max Carey
81. Ty Cobb (1905–28 Tigers and Philadelphia Athletics)
82. Lou Brock
83. Eddie Collins
84. Jim Davenport (San Francisco Giants)
85. Cesar Geronimo (1975–76 Reds)
86. George Brett (Royals)
87. Ralph Kiner (Pirates)
88. Al Rosen (Indians)
89. Mark McGwire (Oakland A's)
90. Diomedes Olivo
91. Warren Spahn (Milwaukee Braves)
92. Denny McLain (1968 Tigers and 1970 Senators)
93. Claude "Lefty" Williams (1919 Chicago Black Sox)
94. George Frazier (Yankees)
95. Johnny Pesky (1942, 1946–47 Red Sox)
96. Tim Raines (White Sox)
97. Karl Spooner
98. J. R. Richard (1978–79)
99. Sandy Koufax (1959 and 1965 Los Angeles Dodgers)
100. Tom Seaver (Mets)

Chapter Six Score

Number of Hits (Correct Answers)   _____
Number of At Bats (Questions)   _____
Season Batting Average   _____

BONUS QUESTION #16
Déjà Vu

The Yankees won the pennant and World Series in 1953. The Indians copped the pennant in 1954.

Both clubs battled down to the wire in 1955, with the Yankees winning their last 15 consecutive games to prevail by three games.

On the Indians side of the field, Bob Feller was winding down, winning just four of eight decisions and striking out just 25 batters. But as "Rapid Robert" was fading, a young but brief meteor was ascending.

The young left-hander won 16 of 26 decisions and struck out 245 batters, an American League record for rookies that still stands.

Who was that "star-struck" phenom? (He now announces the Indians' games.)

A Long Out

The Cleveland Indians won an American League–record 111 games in 1954. But they lost the World Series to the New York Giants in four games. The evolution made baseball followers cognizant of the 1906 Cubs, who had won a record 116 games but lost the Fall Classic to their crosstown rivals, the White Sox, in six games.

The turning point of the 1954 World Series took place in the top of the eighth inning of game one at the Polo Grounds. With two Indians on base, an Indians slugger knocked a pitch 450 feet to the deepest reaches of the Polo Grounds. But Willie Mays made a sensational catch and defused the Indians' rally.

In the bottom of the tenth inning, pinch-hitter Dusty Rhodes hit a three-run homer to decide the game. It also decided the Series. The Indians' morale had been crushed by Mays's catch and Rhodes's homer. It was a game they knew they should have won.

Who was the Indians slugger who hit that ball? (He hit .500 in the Series.) He later contracted polio and battled back from the illness to conclude his career with a .277 lifetime batting average, 266 career homers, and 1,178 total RBIs. Five times he racked up 100 RBI seasons.

BONUS QUESTION #18
Making Their Hits Count

Two Red Sox players during the 1960s won a total of five batting crowns with an average of just .319.

Carl Yastrzemski won three of those batting titles, hitting .321 in 1963, .326 in 1967, and .301 in 1968, the lowest average ever to win a league crown.

But another player, an infielder, won two batting crowns for the Red Sox in the early 1960s. In fact, in five years in Boston, he batted .300 every year, and he averaged .320.

Name that 1960 and 1962 batting champ whom the Red Sox, unbelievably, traded to the Astros for Roman Mejias?

Chapter Seven

Nellie, Harvey, and the Flash

1. Only two National League players have led the league in RBIs for three consecutive years. The first one did it from 1936 to 1938. Who was that Triple Crown winner?
2. The second one did it from 1976 to 1978. Who was that player, who once hit 52 home runs in a season?
3. In his first eight seasons, with the 1922–29 Tigers, this 230-pound outfielder averaged .336. (Over a 12-year career he hit .326.) Who was he?
4. A .313 lifetime hitter, he batted .300 with four teams—the White Sox, Yankees, Cardinals, and Dodgers—and won the 1924 home run title with Brooklyn. Who was he?
5. Name the player who led his loop in at bats a

record 12 years in a row, paced the junior circuit in hits four times, stroked the ball for a .288 average over a 19-year career, broke Joe Morgan in at second base for the Astros, and batted .375 in his only World Series, in 1959?

6. Who hit 30 or more home runs for a record 12 consecutive years? (He hit 534 lifetime.)

7. What Brooklyn Dodgers outfielder hit a record six pinch-hit home runs in one season? (He broke into the majors with batting seasons of .328 and .334 in 1929 and 1930.)

8. Identify the Hall of Famer who played on two world title teams, with one club, in the 1920s, and two Fall Classic champs, with another team, in the 1930s. (He was a .316 lifetime hitter.)

9. A batting titlist in 1953, this Boy of Summer finished his career with a .299 lifetime batting average. (He played on world title teams in 1955 and 1959.) Who was he?

10. Who was the alleged player ringleader of the 1919 Black Sox scandal? (He was the first baseman.)

11. A well-traveled outfielder during his 12-year career, he batted .300 in seasons with the Browns, the Boston Braves, the Pirates, and the Cardinals. (He won the batting crown with the 1940 Pirates.) Who was he?

12. Name the second baseman who hit .280 or better for three consecutive pennant winners. (In 1996 he managed the team for which he played.)

13. Identify the Atlanta Brave of the early 1970s who three times stroked 200 hits in a season,

topping the period off with a batting title in 1974. (He was nicknamed the Road Runner.)

14. What Los Angeles Dodgers player twice recorded 200 hits in three consecutive seasons? (He hit a record four home runs in the 1978 Championship Series.)

15. "Mr. Consistency," he slugged the ball for a .632 percentage in 17 seasons, good for third place on the all-time list. (He punched out a .731 mark in seven World Series as well, garnering a position of third on that all-time list.) Who was he?

16. The "Mechanical Man" hit .320 in 19 regular seasons and .321 in three World Series. (A second baseman, he won the batting title in 1937.) Identify him.

17. "Diamond Jim" once hit 46 home runs and drove home 141 runs in the same season. Who was this Orioles first baseman who finished third behind Roger Maris and Mickey Mantle in the 1961 home run derby?

18. A catcher for 22 years, he is better known as the manager of the 1919 Black Sox. (They called him the Kid.) Who was he?

19. He caught Monte Pearson's no-hitter for the 1937 Yankees and Ted Williams's two innings of relief for the 1940 Red Sox. Can you put the stopper on the "Gabber"? Who was he?

20. During the 1950 season he played every position in the infield and 45 games in the outfield, and he won the American League batting title with a mark of .354. Who was this .300 lifetime hitter?

21. A second baseman, he hit 30 home runs in one

season with the Yankees and 32 in another with the Indians. Who was this player who twice hit .400 in World Series play?

22. An outfielder for the 1947 New York Giants, who hit a National League–record 221 team homers, over a five-year span he knocked out 30, 26, 27, 29, and 25 round-trippers, respectively, for the Giants and the Boston Braves. Who was this .283 lifetime hitter?

23. This catcher was the only player to serve in both World War I and World War II. (He was also the only catcher to hit as high as .545 in a World Series.) Name him.

24. Name the .250-hitting Indians outfielder who went on to broadcast the Indians' games for more than 30 years.

25. Who was the last pitcher to win three games in a World Series? (He also hit his only major-league home run in that Fall Classic.)

26. Two Orioles players ended up in a four-way tie for the 1981 home run title. One of them was Eddie Murray. Who was the other one?

27. A .364 hitter in three World Series with the Cubs, he also managed the Bruins in three Fall Classics (1932, 1935, and 1945), all of which they lost. Tag a name to "Jolly Cholly."

28. Within a span of five years, he played shortstop for two different teams that defeated the Yankees in seven-game World Series. (He won the MVP award in 1960.) Who is he?

29. Name the only Los Angeles Dodgers player to

three times hit 30 home runs in a season. (He added two more in the 1981 World Series.)

30. "Smiling Stan" played all of his 16 years with the same team, batted .301 lifetime, and hit .348 in four World Series. Identify this third baseman (who should be in the Hall of Fame).

31. Who was called the "Kitten" and picked up two wins in seven innings of pitching for the Pirates against the Yankees in the 1960 World Series? (The year before, he "flirted" with a perfect game.)

32. Whose .392 average (50 or more at bats) is the highest in Championship Series play? (His memorable grab against the center field wall in the 1992 World Series started a "near" triple play in game three.)

33. What Orioles relief pitcher performed in three consecutive World Series (1969–71) and picked up a loss despite the fact that he didn't allow an earned run in any of the three Fall Classics? (In two Championship Series with the 1969–70 Orioles, he was 2–0.)

34. A 1963 Twins outfielder hit 33 home runs in his rookie year. He also hit 121 lifetime circuit clouts for six clubs. Who is he?

35. Name the Phillies shortstop who batted .429 in the 1950 World Series against the Yankees but ended his 17-year career as a pitcher for the 1962 Kansas City A's.

36. Who was the journeyman outfielder who pinch-hit for both Ted Williams and Roger Maris? (He batted .225 over eight years.)

37. One player was the only Senator to win two batting titles. (In 1953, he edged Al Rosen by one point, preventing the Indians third baseman from winning the Triple Crown.) Who is he?

38. In his best seasons on the base paths, he stole 35 bases with the 1965 Reds, 38 with the 1970 Brewers, and a club-record 54 with the 1973 Red Sox. (In 1970 he pulled off a 30–30 with Milwaukee.) Who is he?

39. Who was in uniform for each of the Mets' 19 World Series games? (Twice as a player and once as a coach.)

40. He might have been a better golfer than a baseball player, but nevertheless this journeyman first baseman–outfielder hit 35 and 30 home runs in back-to-back years. Name "the Hawk."

41. In the 1924 regular season he batted .268 and hit only one home run; in the 1924 World Series he averaged .333 and drove two round-trippers. Who was this playing manager who led his team to its only world title?

42. A .317 lifetime hitter, he batted .440 and hit three home runs in the 1925 World Series for the losing Senators. (Two years later, he was the first baseman for the Pirates, whom the Yankees swept in the Fall Classic.) Who was he?

43. What San Francisco Giants infielder averaged 28 home runs a season from 1964 to 1968? (He wound up his 12-year career with the 1974 Yankees.)

44. Who was the Cubs great who played on four of four losing teams in the World Series for the

Bruins? (He was a Hall of Famer who batted .297 and hit 236 home runs lifetime. He also was Chicago's manager in the 1938 World Series.)

45. The "Hondo Hurricane" fizzled and hit just 14 home runs in his six-year career with the New York Giants. Who was this "Floppy" outfielder who later unsuccessfully turned to the mound?

46. In his last season this .292 lifetime hitter batted .333 for the Yankees in the 1942 World Series. (Later, he often sang the "Star-Spangled Banner" at Yankee Stadium.) Who was this pre–World War II first baseman?

47. Name the player who caught Bob Feller's 1–0 no-hitter against the Yankees in 1946 and hit a home run to decide the game. (He had a "Blimp" of a day.)

48. Who was the 1941 Indians outfielder who hit for the "Hat Trick": 32 doubles, 20 triples, and 24 home runs? (He homered in every major-league park in existence during his career.)

49. Identify the youngest manager (24) to start a season? (A playing manager, he led his team to a world title the year he won the MVP award.)

50. Name the 1951–53 Yankee who led all American League outfielders in fielding for a record three consecutive years. (He once played on five consecutive world title teams.)

51. Who was the 1929–30 outfielder who batted .381 and .393 but failed to win a batting title? (Lifetime, he hit .324.)

52. A .304 lifetime hitter, this second baseman batted .330 at the age of 34 for the Brooklyn

Dodgers. (A Hall of Famer, he had his best years with the Cubs.) Who was he?

53. Who was the Cardinal who won the 1979 batting title? (He shared the MVP award with Willie Stargell.)

54. Whose 1.000 fielding mark (150 or more games) is the all-time single-season high for a first baseman? (He retired with a record .996 percentage, the same as Wes Parker, who played approximately half the games he did.)

55. In 1945 he led the National League in home runs. Remarkably, he struck out only nine times. Name this .302 lifetime hitter who averaged only 11 strikeouts a year over an 11-year career.

56. A .292 lifetime batter, he hit safely in a record 12 consecutive at bats in 1937. Name this third baseman who played for the Red Sox and later managed them.

57. In 1962 this San Francisco Giant became the first National League player to hit a grand slam in World Series play. Who is he?

58. He played in two World Series, 1955 and 1960, for two underdog teams, the Brooklyn Dodgers and the Pirates, who both won seven-game Series. Name this third baseman.

59. Who hit for the highest average (.373) as a rookie? (He played in two World Series with the Cardinals.)

60. Who played right field in a famous outfield that included Duffy Lewis and Tris Speaker? (He played on four of four world title teams for the Red Sox between 1912 and 1918.)

61. Who was the outfielder–first baseman of the 1940s and 1950s who batted .300 for the Cardinals, the Boston Braves, the Pirates, and the Yankees? (He played in five World Series, three for the Cardinals and two for the Yankees.)

62. What 1988 Oakland A's pitcher got called for a record 16 balks in one season? (He won 20 games in every season from 1987 to 1990.)

63. Identify the successful Yankees manager who played eight years in the majors without hitting a home run or stealing a base. (He won pennants in his first three years of managing, though.)

64. Who played on four losing World Series teams in the 1960s, with two different teams? (He once won the MVP Award.)

65. Who was the 1963 Milwaukee Braves pitcher who got called for a record five balks in one game? (His best season was 1959, when he posted the highest winning percentage (.750) in the American League and split two decisions for the White Sox in the World Series.)

66. Name the deaf outfielder who played 14 years and batted .288 for six clubs. (He was instrumental in getting umpires to raise their arm after called strikes.)

67. Who was the only Yankees manager to die at the helm? (He led the Bombers to three world titles in six tries.)

68. What Tigers pitcher stopped the Yankees' 19-game winning streak in 1947? (The 1906 White

Sox also won 19 consecutive games, the American League record.) He later managed a team against the Yankees in the World Series.

69. This New York Giants outfielder–first baseman batted .458 in the 1951 World Series, but three years later, Leo Durocher, his same skipper in both Series, pinch-hit for him three times. Name this Hall of Famer.

70. Who was the only player to get four doubles in a World Series game? (A second baseman, he played for the "Hitless Wonders.")

71. Whose eight consecutive strikeouts in 1981 set the record of the most by a relief pitcher? (In 1979, his first full season in the majors, he led all American League relief pitchers with 14 wins.)

72. Name the present-day pitcher who struck out 241 batters in 1992, the year he whiffed 18 in one game, and 308 hitters the following year.

73. Can you recall the New York Giants shortstop who batted .291 over a 15-year career and played on World Series–winning teams in 1922 and 1933? (He batted just .149 in four World Series.)

74. From 1919 to 1925 he hit well over .300 in each season for the Browns. Who was the outfielder with the .311 lifetime average?

75. This Indians outfielder batted .300 10 times between 1919 and 1931. (The three times he failed to hit .300, he hit .291.) What was his name?

76. Two left-handers struck out 18 batters in an American League game. Randy Johnson is one of them. Name the retired pitcher who struck

out 248 batters in 1978 but finished second in that category to the Angels' Nolan Ryan's 260.

77. He broke in with the 1950 Yankees; he bowed out with the 1961 Red Sox, with whom he averaged 105 RBIs a year. Who is this 1958 MVP award winner?

78. In 1936 he set a record with 696 official at bats. Who was this Pirates outfielder who batted .285 in nine seasons?

79. Identify the 1950 Rookie of the Year who led the National League in stolen bases his first two years in the majors. (He played just one more year.)

80. "Indian" Bob batted .296 and hit 288 home runs with the Philadelphia Athletics, Senators, and Red Sox. (His brother, Roy, batted .296 also.) What was his surname?

81. In 1972 he hit five home runs with a team in the American League; in 1973 he slammed 43 home runs with a club in the National League. Name this "rags-to-riches" player who is now the manager of the team he played for in 1972.

82. What pitcher struck out a record 181 batters in relief in one season. (In his seven-year career he struck out 51 more batters than he pitched innings.)

83. Identify the player who hit an all-time-high .340 for the Mets one year. (He batted .353 in two Championship Series and .234 in two World Series.)

84. Name the player who was on a World Series

roster five times but never appeared in one Fall Classic. (He played behind Bill Dickey.)

85. Who was the .331 lifetime batter who hit a home run in each of the two 1960 All-Star games, one of them in a pinch-hit role? (He hit 475 lifetime homers but never won a four-base crown.)

86. Identify the .298 lifetime hitter who spent the first 18 years of his 20-year career with the Senators. (In the 1924 World Series, the only Fall Classic that Washington won, this first baseman batted .385.)

87. Name the Hall of Famer who ended his career seven hits above 3,000 and one home run shy of 400. (He was the youngest player, at 20, ever to win a batting title.)

88. He had six 200-hit seasons before 1900 and two after it. Who was this "Hit 'em where they ain't" .345 lifetime hitter?

89. Identify the pitcher who allowed an American League—record 1,775 walks in his career. (Five times during the 1950s he won 20 or more games.)

90. Name the 1939 rookie who hit three home runs in his first World Series. (Over the next five full seasons, he averaged 28 home runs a year. His career was cut short by a back injury.)

91. In the 1920s he hit 20 or more home runs three times, winning the four-base crown in 1921. Who was this New York Giants first baseman? (They called him High Pockets.)

92. Who was the third baseman whose two great plays brought Joe DiMaggio's 56-game hitting

streak to an end in 1941? (He hit a career-high 31 home runs and drove home a career-high 119 runs for the 1948 world title club.)

93. Name the last playing manager. (He led the 1979 White Sox.)

94. Who allowed the fewest hits in three consecutive games? (The "Dutch Master" led the National League in strikeouts from 1941 to 1943.)

95. Name the pitcher who allowed the most grand slams (10) in his career. (He also granted the most walks, 2,795.)

96. Identify the player who hit 30 or more homers in a season with the Cubs, the Mets, and the Oakland A's. (He won two home run titles.)

97. What Phillies long-ball hitter won home run titles in four of his first five years? (He ended his career with an even 300 home runs.)

98. Who was the only Cincinnati Reds player to hit 40 or more homers in three consecutive years? (He did it from 1953 to 1955.)

99. Who was the infielder who starred in the 1926–28 World Series with the Yankees—he hit .500 in the 1927 Fall Classic—and later played in two losing ventures against the Bombers in the postseason?

100. Name the Yankee of the 1950s and 1960s who played four different positions in World Series games. (He later telecast Yankees games.)

Chapter Seven Answers

1. Joe Medwick (Cardinals)
2. George Foster (1978 Reds)
3. Bob Fothergill
4. Jack Fournier
5. Nellie Fox (Philadelphia Athletics, White Sox, and Astros)
6. Jimmie Foxx (1929–40 Philadelphia Athletics and Red Sox)
7. Johnny Frederick
8. Frankie Frisch (1921–22 New York Giants; 1931 and 1934 Cardinals)
9. Carl Furillo (Brooklyn and Los Angeles Dodgers)
10. Chick Gandil
11. Debs Garms
12. Davey Johnson (1969–71 Orioles)
13. Ralph Garr
14. Steve Garvey (1974–76 and 1978–80)
15. Lou Gehrig (Yankees)
16. Charlie Gehringer (Tigers)
17. Jim Gentile (1961)
18. Billy Gleason
19. Joe Glenn

20. Billy Goodman (Red Sox)
21. Joe Gordon (1940 and 1948)
22. Sid Gordon
23. Hank Gowdy (1914 Boston Braves)
24. Jack Graney
25. Mickey Lolich (1968 Tigers)
26. Bobby Grich
27. Charlie Grimm
28. Dick Groat (Pirates and Cardinals)
29. Pedro Guerrero (1982–83 and 1985)
30. Stan Hack (1932–47 Cubs)
31. Harvey Haddix
32. Devon White (1986 Angels and 1991–93 Blue Jays)
33. Dick Hall (1969)
34. Jimmie Hall
35. Granny Hamner
36. Carroll Hardy (Indians and Red Sox)
37. Mickey Vernon (1946 and 1953)
38. Tommy Harper
39. Bud Harrelson (1969 and 1973 as a player; 1986 as a coach)
40. Ken Harrelson (1968–69 Red Sox and Indians)
41. Bucky Harris (Senators)
42. Joe Harris
43. Jim Ray Hart
44. Gabby Hartnett (1929, 1932, 1935, and 1938)
45. Clint Hartung (1947–1952)
46. Buddy Hassett
47. Frank "Blimp" Hayes
48. Jeff Heath
49. Lou Boudreau (1942 and 1948 Indians)

50. Gene Woodling (1949–53)
51. Babe Herman
52. Billy Herman
53. Keith Hernandez
54. Steve Garvey (1984 Padres)
55. Tommy Holmes (Braves)
56. Mike "Pinky" Higgins
57. Chuck Hiller
58. Don Hoak
59. George Watkins (1930 Cardinals)
60. Harry Hooper
61. Johnny Hopp
62. Dave Stewart
63. Ralph Houk (1947–1954; 1961–1963)
64. Elston Howard (1960, 1963–64 Yankees; 1967 Red Sox)
65. Bob Shaw
66. William "Dummy" Hoy
67. Miller Huggins (1929; 1923, 1927–28)
68. Fred Hutchinson (1961 Reds)
69. Monte Irvin (Dusty Rhodes)
70. Frank Isbell (1906 White Sox)
71. Ron Davis (Yankees)
72. Randy Johnson (Mariners)
73. Travis Jackson (1922–1936)
74. William "Baby Doll" Jacobson
75. Charlie Jamieson
76. Ron Guidry (Yankees)
77. Jackie Jensen
78. Woody Jensen
79. Sam Jethroe (1950–52 Boston Braves)
80. Bob Johnson

81. Davey Johnson (Orioles and Atlanta Braves)
82. Dick Radatz (1964 Red Sox)
83. Cleon Jones (1969)
84. Arndt Jorgens
85. Stan Musial (Cardinals)
86. Joe Judge
87. Al Kaline (1955 Tigers)
88. Willie Keeler (Baltimore Orioles and Brooklyn Dodgers)
89. Early Wynn (Indians and White Sox)
90. Charlie Keller
91. George Kelly
92. Kenny Keltner
93. Don Kessinger
94. Johnny Vander Meer (three with the 1938 Reds)
95. Nolan Ryan (1966, 1968–93 Mets, Angels, Astros, and Rangers)
96. Dave Kingman
97. Chuck Klein (1929–33)
98. Ted Kluszewski
99. Mark Koenig (1926–28 Yankees; 1932 Cubs; 1936 New York Giants)
100. Tony Kubek (shortstop, third base, left field, and right field)

Chapter Seven Score

Number of Hits (Correct Answers) _____

Number of At Bats (Questions) _____

Season Batting Average _____

BONUS QUESTION #19
The Monster

The "Green Monster" of a left field wall at Fenway Park in Boston has cast a devastating shadow over pitchers. But during the early 1960s, a six-foot-six, 230-pound right-hander projected an equal fear toward opposing batsmen.

From 1962 to 1964, out of the bull pen, he led relievers in wins every year, ending up with a career-high 16 wins in 1964. In 1962 and 1964, he led the league in saves.

Overall, in seven big-league seasons, he struck out 745 batters in 694 innings.

Who was the pitcher that opposing batters called the "Monster"?

BONUS QUESTION #20
Speaking of Shortstops

See if you can identify the following Hall of Famer:

He played all 18 years of his major-league career at one position. In 1956, with the White Sox, he won the Rookie of the Year award. From 1956 to 1964 he copped a major league–record nine consecutive stolen base titles. In addition, he played in World Series with the losing 1959 White Sox and the winning 1966 Orioles.

Who was this .262 lifetime hitter who played all 2,581 of his games in the field at shortstop?

BONUS QUESTION #21
The Year of the Pitcher

The 1968 season was "the Year of the Pitcher."

Denny McLain of the Tigers won 31 games to become the first 30-game winner since Dizzy Dean of the 1934 Cardinals spun a 30–7 record.

Bob Gibson of the Cardinals paced the majors with an ERA of 1.12. It has been the lowest mark turned in by a starting pitcher since World War II. Bob Bolin of the San Francisco Giants finished in runner-up position with a 1.99 log.

The five lowest pitchers in ERA in the American League were all under the 2.00 mark: Luis Tiant of the Indians (1.60), Sam McDowell of the Indians (1.81), Dave McNally of the Orioles (1.95), Denny McLain of the Tigers (1.96), and Tommy John of the White Sox (1.98).

That was the year Don Drysdale of the Los Angeles Dodgers spun a record six consecutive shutouts, breaking the 64-year-old major-league record of Doc White of the 1904 White Sox, who hurled five consecutive shutouts.

Drysdale also broke another record in 1968, that of Walter Johnson's 56 consecutive scoreless innings with the 1913 Senators. Drysdale went 2⅔ innings beyond the "Big Train's" mark.

Twenty years later, however, Drysdale's mark was eclipsed by a third of an inning. Who was that Cy Young Award winner of 1988 who broke "Big Don's" record? He has an 8–1 career postseason mark.

Chapter Eight

Christy, Sparky, and the Babe

1. Who was the only pitcher to win the Cy Young Award in both leagues? (At 40, he was the oldest hurler to win it.)
2. Name the team that batted .338 in a World Series, the all-time high, but lost that Fall Classic in seven games.
3. Who was the oldest player in the National League to win a batting title? (At 37, he won the last of his league-record eight hitting crowns.)
4. Do you recall the oldest person (59) to play in the majors? (In 1948 he was a 41-year-old rookie.)
5. Who was the 1962–82 player with a record 150 safeties as a pinch hitter? (Careerwise, he batted

.304 with the San Francisco Giants, the Pirates, the Expos, and the Los Angeles Dodgers.)

6. Two players got a record 230 hits in one year as switch-hitters. Willie Wilson of the 1980 Royals did it in the American League. Who was the 1973 MVP who did it in the National League?

7. Name the player who batted safely in a rookie-record 34 consecutive games. (He won the Rookie of the Year award that year.)

8. Who was the only player to twice hit three home runs in a World Series game? (He performed that feat only once during regular-season play.)

9. Did Roger Maris win one, two, or three home run crowns?

10. Name the catcher who grounded into season-high double plays a record five times. (A Hall of Famer, he batted .306 lifetime.)

11. He didn't win his first game until he was 31, but in 1935 he ended his career with 197. Who was this Hall of Famer?

12. Identify the first baseman who didn't make an error in a record 193 consecutive games. (He played in four World Series with one National League club and one Fall Classic with another senior circuit team.)

13. Name the 1949–53 right fielder for the Yankees who played on five consecutive world-title teams. (Lifetime, he batted .277.)

14. Name the 1908 Indians pitcher who on the next-to-last day of the season pitched a perfect game on the same afternoon that his mound adver-

sary, Ed Walsh of the White Sox, hurled a two-hitter? (He registered a career 1.88 ERA, second to Walsh's 1.82.)

15. What pitcher threw the most innings in a one-hit effort? (He was 2–0 with a 2.45 ERA in the 1960 World Series.)

16. What Red Sox player averaged 147 RBIs a season from 1948–50? (Earlier, he won an RBIs title, 1944, and a home run crown, 1945, with the Browns.)

17. Was it Tom Seaver, Lefty Grove, Dazzy Vance, or Walter Johnson who won a record eight consecutive strikeout titles?

18. Identify the only black man to play in World Series in his first four years in the majors. (He hit a home run in his first Fall Classic at bat.)

19. Can you remember the only pitcher to throw no-hitters in each of his first two years in the majors? (He did it with the 1972–73 Royals.)

20. Who became the first National League player to hit 40 home runs in a season? (He hit 301 lifetime.)

21. Name the last of the legal spitball pitchers. (This 1934 Yankee, Pirate, and Cardinal won 270 career games.)

22. Who was the last of the legal spitball pitchers in the American League? (This 1933 White Sox pitcher once won three games in a World Series.)

23. Whose 23 consecutive hitless innings as a starting pitcher in 1904 tops even Johnny Vander Meer's 21 consecutive no-hit innings in 1938, the year of his record back-to-back no-hit games?

(The Red Sox hurler pitched this century's first perfect game that year.)

24. Whose first hit was a grand slam off the Brooklyn Dodgers' Carl Erskine in 1954? (A Phillie, he got only three more hits in the majors.)

25. Name the one-time coach for John McGraw, with whom he played with the Orioles, who later managed Brooklyn to two pennants.

26. Who was the two-time home run champ who lost his job to Lou Gehrig? (He averaged 10 triples a year over a 15-year career.)

27. What 1973 Oakland A's second baseman was fired by Charlie Finley because he made two errors in the twelfth inning of a World Series loss to the Mets? (Commissioner Bowie Kuhn forced Finley to reinstate this player.)

28. Who was the player who averaged 240 hits a season from 1920 to 1922, including a record 257 in 1920? (This Hall of Famer never played in a World Series.)

29. Who pitched a record seven shutouts in opening game starts? (In 1909, he lost by shutout a record five times during one month.)

30. Name the only pitcher to twice lead his league in saves and complete games in the same season. (He pitched in four World Series with the Cubs.)

31. Identify the pitcher of the 1950s and 1960s who won 19 games a record four times. (In 1957, he won 20 games with the Tigers.)

32. Who was the first player to appear in one World Series as a pitcher and another as an outfielder?

(He won three games for the 1912 Red Sox and batted .200 for the 1920 Indians.)

33. Name the American League outfielder who averaged 118 RBIs per season for 13 years but won only two titles in that category. (Over his first five years he averaged one RBI a game.)

34. What 1971 Phillies pitcher hurled a no-hitter and hit two home runs in a win over the Reds? (This 188-game career winner copped a victory in both the Championship Series and the World Series for the 1975 Red Sox, when he won 19 games in his best season.)

35. Do you remember the Hall of Fame infielder who hit into a record four triple plays? (He twice hit .500 in Championship Series.)

36. Whose 28 wins in one year in the 1950s represents the most single-season victories by any National League pitcher since Dizzy Dean of the Cardinals won 30 in 1934? (He won 286 career games.)

37. An eight-time 20-game winner, he once lost a record 29 games in one season. (He lost them with the Boston Braves.) Who was he?

38. Which of the following teams did not come back from a 3–1 deficit to win a World Series: 1925 Pirates, 1947 Yankees, 1958 Yankees, 1968 Tigers, 1979 Pirates, or 1985 Royals?

39. Honus Wagner, Ty Cobb, Babe Ruth, Walter Johnson, and which other person were the first five players to be inducted into the Hall of Fame at Cooperstown in 1936?

40. Which pitcher set a National League record

when he won seven consecutive strikeout crowns? (He didn't win his first game until he was 31.)

41. Name the 17-year pitcher, notably with the Indians and the Tigers, who won an even 200 games and batted .288, a record for a full-time moundsman. (He won his 200th game with the 1934 Yankees.)

42. Identify the 1939 Yankee who scored at least one run in each of a record 18 consecutive games. (He later managed the Tigers and served as the athletic director at Dartmouth College.)

43. Whose first major-league home run was the longest up until that point in the history of Royals Stadium? (He won the Heisman Trophy while he was at Auburn.)

44. Name the 1992–93 Mets pitcher who lost a record 27 consecutive games. (The previous high was 19 by Jack Nabors of the 1916 Philadelphia Athletics.)

45. Whose 57 saves for the 1990 White Sox is a record? (He averaged 39 saves a season from 1988 to 1991.)

46. Baseball's three greatest home run hitters—Hank Aaron, Babe Ruth, and Willie Mays—each ended his career in the same city in which he started it, but with different franchises. Name the respective clubs.

47. Who was the old-time player who hit only eight home runs in 1911 but drove home 144 runs, a record number for a player with less than 10 round-trippers? (He hit .420 that year.)

48. Who lost the most games (16) in one year as a relief pitcher? (He was one of the two Atlanta Braves pitchers who combined to stop Pete Rose's 44-game hitting streak in 1978.)

49. Who in 1901 batted .422, the highest single-season average in the history of the American League? (He batted .339 lifetime and won three batting titles.)

50. What player in 1951 became the first of three American League pitchers to throw two no-hitters in one season? (Virgil Trucks of the 1952 Tigers and Nolan Ryan of the 1973 Angels did it also.)

51. Name the first right-handed batter to get 200 hits in five consecutive seasons. (He won batting titles in 1930 and 1931.)

52. One pitcher won a record 19 consecutive games in one season. (He won 26 games that season and copped two more in the World Series.) Who was he?

53. What player hit for the cycle three times, the American League high? (He won the home run crown in 1925.)

54. Name the player who hit for the cycle three times, the National League high. (A .324 lifetime hitter, he never won a batting title.)

55. Zero in on the 1974–76 San Francisco Giants and Padres pitcher who won the most games (12) of any relief pitcher from the start of his career? (He won just six more games over the rest of his career.)

56. Name the Phillies player who collected 200 hits

in each season from 1929 to 1933. (He won a Triple Crown.)

57. Who was the 1972 Padres player who hit five home runs in a doubleheader? (The only other player to perform that feat was Stan Musial of the 1954 Cardinals.)

58. Who twice had a record six hits in six at bats in the National League? (In his first 10 seasons he batted .300 every year except 1926, when he hit .299.)

59. What player hit a National League–record 101 home runs in back-to-back years? (He twice tied for home run crowns with Johnny Mize of the New York Giants, in 1947 and 1948.)

60. Who reached a one-league record of 18 pinch-hit home runs? (He played for the Reds and the Pirates.)

61. Name the manager who won nine pennants—one in the National League and eight in the American League—and never finished lower than fourth in the standings.

62. What player hit a National League–record 34 home runs at his home grounds one year? (From 1953 to 1955 he averaged 45 circuit clouts per campaign.)

63. Identify the pitcher who twice hit seven home runs in a season, the National League high. (A Hall of Famer, he won 209 career games, including an all-time-high 25 in 1962.)

64. Name the pitcher who hit a career-high 38 home runs and a single-season-high 9 circuit clouts for a player at his position. (Six times he won 20

games, four times with the Indians and twice with the Red Sox.)

65. Who hit for a record 25 total bases in two consecutive games? (He also hit for a record 18 in one game.)

66. Name the six-time home run champ who hit more right-handed home runs (586) than any other player except Hank Aaron and Willie Mays.

67. What pitcher has a .690 winning percentage, a record for hurlers with 200 or more victories? (He had a 2.75 regular-season ERA and a 2.71 World Series ERA.)

68. Name the 22–3 winner for the Brooklyn Dodgers who posted a National League–record .880 winning percentage one year. (In the 1949 World Series he outdueled Vic Raschi of the Yankees, 1–0.)

69. After the Giants traded him to the Cubs, he promptly proved that his former team had made a mistake by winning three home run titles in his first three years in the Windy City. Name him.

70. Name the 1991 Mets right-hander who struck out a National League record-tying 19 batters in one game. (He won the Cy Young Award in the American League.)

71. Who was the 1946 player who stole home a record seven times in one season? (He never stole home before or after that season.)

72. Name the Yankees relief pitcher who won an American League–record 12 consecutive games

in relief one year. (He led the league with 15 wins and 29 saves out of the bull pen.)

73. Whose life does the movie *Fear Strikes Out* document? (A good defensive outfielder for 17 years, he hit his 100th career homer with the 1963 Mets and celebrated the occasion running the bases backward.)

74. Two American League pitchers won a loop-record 17 consecutive games. Who was the Indians hurler? (His .938 winning percentage is a junior circuit mark for hurlers with at least 15 decisions.)

75. Who was the Orioles pitcher? (He won 20 or more games from 1968 to 1971.)

76. Identify the pitcher who won 23 consecutive games from the Philadelphia Athletics. (He posted 20-win seasons with the Red Sox, the Yankees, and the Reds.)

77. In World Series play he won four of four decisions for a West Coast team and one of four for an East Coast club. Who is he?

78. What American League switch-hitter got 100 hits from each side of the plate in 1980? (He stole 79 bases that year.)

79. Who was the National League switch-hitter who got 100 hits from each side of the plate in 1979? (He led his league in triples his first three years in the majors.)

80. In 1904 he set a record when he struck out 349 opposing batters. That American League mark stood until Nolan Ryan of the 1973 Angels

struck out 383 batters. Name the four-time 20-game winner.

81. Pinpoint the pitcher who appeared in 899 games, all in relief. (He won the Cy Young Award in 1977.)

82. Who won three batting titles with a combined average of .315? (He once won the Triple Crown.)

83. Who was the right-handed batter who got 253 hits in a season, a record for a hitter from that side of the plate? (He drove home 100 runs in each of his first 11 seasons in the majors.)

84. Identify the National League second baseman who got a record seven hits in a nine-inning game. (He had his best year in 1977, when he batted .336.)

85. Who collected a record five hits in his first major-league game? (He suffered from frostbite of the toes in World War II.)

86. Name the Hall of Famer who collected one or more long hits in a record 14 consecutive games. (He won batting titles in 1927, 1934, and 1936.)

87. Which pitcher set a record, since tied by Dale Mahorcik of the 1986 Rangers, when he pitched 13 consecutive games in relief? (That year he appeared in a record 106 games as a pitcher.)

88. Identify the Cubs player who drove home at least one run in a record 17 consecutive games. (A .329 lifetime hitter, he had a twin brother, Roy, and a son, Oscar, who played in the majors.)

89. Whose 11 seasons of 300 or more innings

pitched is a record? (His .665 career winning percentage is a league record, too.)

90. Whose 15 opening-day starts is a single-league record? (He ended his career with a National League–high 4,000 strikeouts. He added 131 strikeouts in the American League.)

91. Name the only player to hit a grand slam in his first major-league game. (He has a son who plays in the majors today.)

92. Name the part-time player who hit four consecutive homers in three consecutive games. (He played in five consecutive World Series for the Yankees, batting .345.)

93. Who was the only pitcher to hit three home runs in a game? (He lost a league-leading 21 games for the Boston Braves that year.)

94. Who stopped Ty Cobb's streak of nine consecutive batting titles when he led the league with a .386 average in 1916. (He player-managed the Indians to the world title in 1920.)

95. This early-century Cubs and Cardinals pitcher completed 98 percent of his starts. (He started 286 games and finished 278 of them.) Who was he?

96. Who was the designated hitter-utility player who hit a record 20 pinch-hit home runs? (He played in the 1977–78 World Series with the Yankees.)

97. Name the only player who two times in a season legged out three triples in a game. (In 1907, with the Boston Braves, he led the National League in home runs.)

98. Identify the Hall of Famer who sprayed a record

198 singles in his rookie season. (He collected 200 or more hits in his first three years in the majors, 1927–29.) Johnny Pesky was the only other player to get 200 or more hits in his first three seasons.

99. Who was the player who set a record when he reached base 16 consecutive times? (He was 39 at the time.)

100. This Pirates outfielder slammed a record 36 triples in 1912. (For the eight other years of his career, he averaged nine per season.) Who was he?

Chapter Eight Answers

1. Gaylord Perry (1972 Indians and 1978 Padres)
2. 1960 Yankees (Pirates)
3. Honus Wagner (1911 Pirates)
4. Satchel Paige (with the 1965 Kansas City Athletics; 1948 Indians)
5. Manny Mota
6. Pete Rose (Reds)
7. Benito Santiago (1987 Padres)
8. Babe Ruth (1926 and 1928 Yankees)
9. One (1961 Yankees)
10. Ernie Lombardi
11. Dazzy Vance
12. Steve Garvey (1983–85 Padres; 1974, 1977–78, 1981 Los Angeles Dodgers, 1984 Padres)
13. Hank Bauer
14. Addie Joss
15. Harvey Haddix (1959 Pirates; 12⅓ against the Milwaukee Braves)
16. Vern Stephens
17. Walter Johnson (1912–19 Senators)
18. Elston Howard (1955–58 Yankees)
19. Steve Busby

20. Rogers Hornsby (42 with 1922 Cardinals)
21. Burleigh Grimes
22. Red Faber (1917)
23. Cy Young (Red Sox)
24. Jim Command
25. Wilbert Robinson
26. Wally Pipp (1916–17)
27. Mike Andrews
28. George Sisler (Browns)
29. Walter Johnson (1907–27 Senators)
30. Mordecai "Three Finger" Brown (1909–10 Cubs)
31. Jim Bunning
32. "Smoky" Joe Wood
33. Joe DiMaggio (1941 and 1948)
34. Rick Wise
35. Brooks Robinson (1969–70 Orioles—.500 and .583)
36. Robin Roberts (1952 Phillies)
37. Vic Willis (1905)
38. 1947 Yankees
39. Christy Mathewson (New York Giants and Reds)
40. Dazzy Vance
41. George Uhle
42. Red Rolfe
43. Bo Jackson
44. Anthony Young
45. Bobby Thigpen
46. Aaron (Milwaukee Braves–Brewers), Ruth (Boston Red Sox–Braves), and Mays (New York Giants–Mets)
47. Ty Cobb (Tigers)

48. Gene Garber (Larry McWilliams was the other hurler; 1979)
49. Nap Lajoie (1901 Philadelphia Athletics and 1903–4 Cleveland Indians)
50. Allie Reynolds (Yankees)
51. Al Simmons (1929–33 Philadelphia Athletics)
52. Rube Marquard (1912 New York Giants)
53. Bob Meusel (Yankees)
54. Babe Herman (Brooklyn Dodgers and Cubs)
55. Butch Metzger
56. Chuck Klein (1933)
57. Nate Colbert
58. Jim Bottomley (Cardinals)
59. Ralph Kiner (1949–50 Pirates)
60. Jerry Lynch
61. Joe McCarthy (1929 Cubs; 1932, 1936–39, 1941–43 Yankees)
62. Ted Kluszewski (1954 Reds)
63. Don Drysdale (1958, 1965 Los Angeles Dodgers)
64. Wes Ferrell (1931 Indians)
65. Joe Adcock (1954 Milwaukee Braves)
66. Harmon Killebrew (Senators, Twins and Royals)
67. Whitey Ford
68. Preacher Roe (1951 Brooklyn Dodgers)
69. Hack Wilson
70. David Cone (1994 Royals)
71. Pete Reiser (Brooklyn Dodgers)
72. Luis Arroyo (1961)
73. Jimmy Piersall
74. Johnny Allen (1936–37)
75. Dave McNally (1968–69)
76. Carl Mays

77. Jim Hunter (1972–74 A's; 1976–78 Yankees)
78. Willie Wilson (Royals)
79. Garry Templeton (Cardinals)
80. Rube Waddell (1902–05 Philadelphia Athletics)
81. Sparky Lyle
82. Carl Yastrzemski (1963, 1967–68 Red Sox; 1967)
83. Al Simmons (1925 Philadelphia Athletics)
84. Rennie Stennett (1975 Pirates)
85. Cecil Travis (1933 Senators)
86. Paul Waner (1927 Pirates)
87. Mike Marshall (1974 Los Angeles Dodgers)
88. Ray Grimes (1992 Cubs)
89. Christy Mathewson (1900–1916 New York Giants and Reds, with whom he won one game in 1916)
90. Steve Carlton
91. Bobby Bonds (Barry)
92. Johnny Blanchard (1961 Yankees)
93. Jim Tobin (1942)
94. Tris Speaker (Indians)
95. Jack Taylor (1898–1907)
96. Cliff Johnson
97. Dave Brain
98. Lloyd Waner (1927 Pirates)
99. Ted Williams (1957 Red Sox)
100. Owen Wilson

Chapter Eight Score

Number of Hits (Correct Answers) _____
Number of At Bats (Questions) _____
Season Batting Average _____

The Reserve Clause

A very good ballplayer sat out the 1970 season because he refused to be traded from his team to the Phillies without his permission.

Over 15 years he batted .293 with a high of .335 in 1967, and he delivered a league-high 211 hits in 1965. He played in three World Series, twice on the winning side. He thought that his team of 12 years had been disloyal to him, so he tested the reserve clause, which restricted a player's right to offer his services to the highest bidder. Baseball owners had for years successfully argued that if the reserve clause were abolished, all of the best players would end up with the richest teams.

The player who led the National League in at bats in both 1963 and 1964 took his suit all the way to the Supreme Court before it was denied. The court ruled that the reserve clause was legal because baseball remained exempt from antitrust laws, but it found this exemption an "aberration" and asked Congress to look into it, since the National Pastime clearly is a business.

Pitchers Andy Messersmith and Dave McNally

challenged the reserve clause again, in December 1975. They challenged it not from a legal standpoint but from a contractual dispute. Arbitrator Peter M. Seitz ruled that they were free agents. He concluded that a player's contract cannot be renewed repeatedly until the player is sold, traded, released, or retires. Messersmith subsequently signed with the Braves and became baseball's first "millionaire."

But the player who set the stage for the defeat of the reserve clause back in 1970 never profited from its demise and the super salaries that came about as the result of its abolishment. Who was that outstanding all-round player?

BONUS QUESTION #23
The Secretary of Defense

Up until 1980, the Phillies didn't have much luck in the World Series. They had appeared in two Fall Classics, 1915 and 1950, and registered just one win, a 3–1 victory by Grover Cleveland Alexander over the Red Sox in the opening game of the former World Series.

They seemed to be snakebit. That jinx continued during the 1976–78 playoffs. They lost to the Reds in 1976, and they bowed to the Los Angeles Dodgers in both 1977 and 1978.

But the way they lost in 1978 punctuated their futility. With the Dodgers leading in games, 2–1, the Phillies' usually sure-handed center fielder dropped an easy fly ball, and Bill Russell followed with a game-winning and Championship Series–winning single.

Harry Kalas, the voice of the Phillies, used to say, "Two-thirds of the earth is covered by water, and the other one-third is covered by the Secretary of Defense."

Who was that "Secretary of Defense"?

BONUS QUESTION #24
They Could Hit

Two batters in the history of the game have compiled the highest single-season average for at least two teams.

Rogers Hornsby hit .424 with the 1924 Cardinals, .387 with the 1928 Braves, and .380 with the 1929 Cubs to pace those three franchises. Overall, he won seven batting titles.

In the American League, a more recent player batted .388 with one team and .339 with another club to highlight two different clubs.

Who was this player, who also won seven batting crowns?

Chapter Nine

Jackie, Barry, and the Goose

1. Name the Los Angeles Dodgers pitcher who posted an 11–0 record at Dodger Stadium in 1985. (He won the Cy Young Award in 1988.)
2. The Los Angeles Dodgers of the mid-1960s had an infield that was composed of four switch-hitters: third baseman Jim Gilliam, shortstop Maury Wills, second baseman Jim Lefebvre, and which first baseman?
3. Before Tony Gwynn of the 1987–89 Padres won three consecutive batting titles, who was the last National League player to win three straight hitting crowns? (Overall, he won seven.)
4. Padres pitchers won two Cy Young awards between 1976 and 1978. Randy Jones won it in

1976. The hurler who won it in 1978 was a 314-game lifetime winner. Who is he?

5. Which Padres pitcher was suspended in 1986 for criticizing owner Ray Kroc's product? (Kroc was the owner of McDonald's.)

6. In the Giants' first two years in San Francisco (1958–59), two of their players won Rookie of the Year. Who was the first? (Later, he won the MVP award with the 1967 Cardinals.)

7. Who was the second? (He won the 1969 MVP award with the Giants.)

8. Two teams have had four 20-game winners on their staffs. The first one was the 1920 White Sox, who had Red Faber, Claude "Lefty" Williams, Ed Cicotte, and which other 20-win hurler?

9. The other club was the 1971 Orioles, who had four 20-win pitchers in Dave McNally, Pat Dobson, Mike Cuellar, and which other 20-victory hurler?

10. Name the 1978 MVP winner who set another, though dubious, mark when he later grounded into a season-record 36 double plays. (He won three home run crowns with the Red Sox.)

11. Who was the regular first baseman for the 1947 pennant-winning Brooklyn Dodgers? (He moved to second base the following season.)

12. What 1953 Indians player missed winning the Triple Crown by one batting point? (In his seven full years he averaged 102 RBIs per season.)

13. Who was the only Indians pitcher to post a 30-win season? (His son was one of the two Tribe

pitchers who stopped Joe DiMaggio's batting streak in 1941.)

14. Name the catcher who received six different 20-game winners during his years with the Indians. (His son Mike played 12 years in the major leagues.)

15. Which of the following Tigers was the last to win a batting title: George Kell, Harvey Kuenn, Al Kaline, or Norm Cash?

16. Who was the only Yankees pitcher to win the MVP award? (His winning percentage of .717 is the all-time high for pitchers with at least 100 career victories.)

17. Name the only regular player to three times hit .400 in the World Series. (At one point, this infielder hit .300 for eight consecutive years; at another point, he batted .300 for 10 consecutive seasons.)

18. Identify the White Sox pitcher who led the league in losses the year after he won the Cy Young Award. (He led the American League in wins in both 1982 and 1983 before finishing his career with the 1986 Padres.)

19. Name the Tigers pitcher who tied an American League record by winning 16 consecutive games in 1934. (He won 24 games during the regular season and split two contests in the World Series.)

20. Name the catcher who stole 36 bases in 1982, a record for a player at his position. (In five American League Championship Series he didn't get a hit.)

21. Who was the first black pitcher to win a World Series game? (He was 15–4 in his Rookie of the Year award season; he was 15–8 over the rest of his career.)

22. Who was the first black pitcher to win two games in a World Series? (He had his best season, 21–7, in 1965, the year he won those postseason contests.)

23. Who was the only black pitcher to win three games in a World Series? (The following year, he hurled 13 shutouts, second highest on the all-time list, after Grover Alexander, who spun a record-high 16 blankings in one season.)

24. Which 1969 slugger smacked an all-time-high 37 home runs by the All-Star Game break? (He finished the season with 47 circuit clouts.)

25. He played with the Oakland A's for three seasons (1984–86), and he hit 30 or more home runs in each of them. (The following year, he was released, and he never again played in the majors.) Who is he?

26. Which Oakland A's manager was the only skipper in the history of baseball to be traded for a player? (He led the Pirates to the world title in 1979.)

27. What relief pitcher hurled a record 185 consecutive innings without issuing a base on balls? (He was 20–8 for the 1978 Red Sox.)

28. Who was the only pitcher to perform in each contest of a seven-game World Series? (His ERA was 0.00.)

29. Name the outfielder of the 1970s and 1980s who

batted .300 with the Angels, the Yankees, and the Rangers. (He stole a club-high 70 bases with the 1975 Angels.)

30. Identify the catcher of the 1950s who won three MVP titles in alternate years. (He hit 242 lifetime homers, breaking Gabby Hartnett's previous high of 236 at his position.)

31. Who was the first black pitcher to win the Cy Young Award? (A 27-game winner, he copped it in the first year of its existence. But he lost the seventh game of that year's World Series.)

32. Name the only black player to win the Triple Crown. (He batted only .316, but he hit 49 home runs and drove home 122 runs.)

33. Identify the first black player to win the MVP award in the American League. (He hit a home run in his first World Series at bat in 1955.)

34. Who was the first black player to win the MVP award? (He batted .342, stole a career-high 37 bases, and drove home a career-high 124 runs, the only time that he topped the 100 mark.)

35. What player was the only black pitcher to twice strike out 300 batters in a season? (His career was cut short by a stroke.)

36. Identify the only other black pitcher to strike out 300 batters in a season. (He did it in 1971, when he won the Cy Young Award.)

37. Which black pitcher won a record seven consecutive games in the World Series? (In 1968, he struck out a record 17 batters in one Fall Classic contest.)

38. Who was the only Tigers pitcher to win Rookie

of the Year? (He won 19 games that year, nine more than he copped over the rest of his career.)

39. Who was the only black player to perform in four different decades? (He hit 521 career homers.)

40. Name the first black player to win back-to-back batting championships. (A .294 lifetime hitter, he played with a record 10 different teams.)

41. The first black player to perform in the American League was also the first black to win two home run titles. Who is he?

42. Who was the only player to win the MVP award in both leagues? (He hit eight World Series home runs.)

43. Four black players have won back-to-back MVP awards. Name the shortstop who averaged 44 home runs a year from 1958 to 1960.

44. Who was the Brewers outfielder who tied Reggie Jackson for the home run title in 1980. (He hit 235 career homers with the Red Sox, the Tigers, and the Brewers)

45. Who was the Brewers outfielder who tied Reggie Jackson for the home run crown in 1982? (He won another four-base title, in 1979.)

46. Who was the first black pitcher to throw a no-hitter? (That year he led his league in losses, with 20; walks, with 185; and strikeouts, with 198.)

47. Who was the first black to manage in the majors? (He was also the first black to manage in the National League.)

48. Who hit 475 homers, won two four-base titles,

and got 12 hits in the 1979 World Series, the year he won the MVP award?

49. Who was on deck when Bobby Thomson hit the pennant-winning home run for the 1951 New York Giants? (He went on to win home run crowns in 1955, 1962, 1964, and 1965.)

50. Whose injury in the 1937 All-Star Game cut short his dazzling career? (Hall of Famer Earl Averill hit the line drive that broke this player's toe.)

51. Who was the first player to hit two home runs in an All-Star Game? (A shortstop, he once hit .385 in a season.)

52. Who gave up his first and only *eephus* pitch home run in the 1946 All-Star Game? (Ted Williams hit it.)

53. Name the Cubs hurler whose six strikeouts in the 1967 All-Star Game tied the record set by Carl Hubbell of the 1934 New York Giants and equaled by Johnny Vander Meer of the 1943 Reds.

54. Identify the player—he was not even listed on that year's All-Star Game ballot—who was the MVP in the 1974 game. (He was elected as a write-in candidate.)

55. Name the 1976–78 Yankee who batted .386 in three Championship Series and .238 in three World Series. (He stole 43 bases for the 1976 Yankees.)

56. Who was the only pitcher to hit a grand slam in a Championship Series? (He was 2–2 in five

Championship Series and 2–2 in three World Series with the Orioles.)

57. The only pitcher to hit a grand slam in the World Series was who? (He went 21–5 in 1971 to lead the American League with an .808 winning percentage.)

58. Who was the youngest player (19) to pitch in a Championship Series? (Overall, he was 3–0 with the Pirates and the Twins.)

59. Name the pitcher who lost a record seven consecutive games in Championship Series play. (He never won a Championship Series game, but he defeated Ron Guidry of the Yankees in a key World Series contest.)

60. Who hit safely in a record 17 consecutive World Series games? (He also hit seven home runs, the second highest total by a right-handed batter.)

61. Who played on the winning World Series team a record 10 times? (He played in a record 14 Fall Classics.)

62. Name the National League player who was on the losing World Series team a National League record six times. (A Hall of Famer, he was an infielder.)

63. Identify the player who was in the World Series five times and ended up on the losing club on each occasion. (He is best remembered for a base-running mistake that cost the 1908 New York Giants the pennant.)

64. What player from the 1930s had a career World Series batting average of .418, the all-time high for a player with at least 50 at bats. (He stole

seven bases, five in 1931 and two in 1934, off the same Hall of Fame catcher.)

65. Name the Yankees shortstop who was given his release on Old Timers' Day? (He once won the MVP Award.)

66. Who once hit four home runs in a four-game World Series? (In his next Series, he hit three home runs in a four-game Classic.)

67. Name the player from the 1980s who struck out a record 12 times in one World Series. (Two years later, he won a batting crown.)

68. Identify the pitcher who won five consecutive World Series games during the 1960, 1961, and 1962 Fall Classics. (He spun a record 33⅔ consecutive scoreless innings during that span.)

69. What Yankees player once hit two home runs in the seventh game of a World Series win? (He hit them off Don Newcombe of the Brooklyn Dodgers.)

70. Name the 1990 Reds infielder who batted .563 in the World Series, the third all-time high, and got eight hits in his last 11 at bats. (He won the 1988 Rookie of the Year award.)

71. Reach back to pinpoint the man who pitched a record three shutouts in one World Series. (He walked only one batter in 27 innings of pitching.) Who was he?

72. Whom did Don Larsen catch looking for the last out of his perfect game? (It was the last at bat of an 11-year career in which he struck out an average of just 11 times a season.)

73. Who umpired behind the plate the day Larsen

pitched his perfect game? (It was the last game he ever umpired behind the plate.)

74. Who was the Red Sox pitcher who allowed just four hits in two winning World Series games against the 1967 Cardinals? (He won the Cy Young Award that year.)

75. Name the youngest pitcher (20) to throw a shutout in the World Series. (He did it in 1966.)

76. Identify the pitcher who hurled a record 14–inning win against the Brooklyn Dodgers in a World Series game. (He gave up a run in the first inning of the 2–1 contest and then chalked up 13⅓ consecutive shutout innings.)

77. Who was the losing pitcher who went the distance in that game? (His 0.89 ERA is the fourth all-time best in Series play.)

78. What Cardinals pitcher of the 1940s was 4–1 in World Series play? (His 0.83 ERA in Series play is the second all-time best.)

79. Which White Sox pitcher with the 1919 Black Sox won 20 games and both of his contests in that year's World Series? (Following a contract dispute in 1921, he sat out three consecutive years and never won another game in the majors.)

80. Who was the Yankees pitcher that didn't allow an earned run in 27 innings of pitching in the 1927 World Series but lost one of his three decisions? (He lost the final contest of the eight-game Series on an error, 1–0.)

81. Who umpired the most World Series games (104), the most Fall Classics (18), and the most

consecutive Series (5)? (He once said, "I never missed a call in my life.")

82. Whose bad-hop single in the 1924 World Series gave the Senators their only world title? (He was a rookie who hit .330 in limited play.)

83. Whose tenth-inning homer in game five of the 1933 World Series won the championship for the New York Giants? (This outfielder with more than 500 career home runs hit a two-run, four-base blow that was the margin of difference in game one, too.)

84. Whose 6–1 victory in game one of the 1936 World Series ended a Yankee 12-game winning streak in postseason play? (He won 20 games a season from 1933 to 1937.)

85. The Yankees won 20 of 23 Fall Classic contests in the 1930s. One National League pitcher defeated them twice, though. Who was he?

86. Name the other pitcher who defeated the Bronx Bombers in the 1930s. (Also a Giant, he won a total of 42 games in 1934 and 1935 and split four games in Series play.)

87. Identify the Yankees pitcher of the 1930s who won four games without a defeat in World Series play. (He won one game in each of four consecutive Series. He also no-hit the Indians in 1937.)

88. A Brooklyn Dodger, he broke the Yankees' 10-game World Series winning streak in 1941. (He won 22 games that year.) Who was he?

89. Name the only pitcher to split four decisions in a World Series. (A 20-game winner that year, he

also split the season between the Yankees and the pennant-winning Cubs.)

90. Whose three-run triple and sliding catch to end the game made the difference in the final contest between the Yankees and the New York Giants in the 1951 World Series? (In the 1958 World Series he hit home runs in a record-tying three consecutive games.)

91. Name the Yankees part-time player in 1952 who set a World Series record when he hit a homer in each of three consecutive games. (A .312 lifetime hitter, he won four home run crowns in the National League.)

92. Who was the Brooklyn right-hander who whiffed a then-record 14 batters in a 1953 World Series game? (He fanned Mickey Mantle and Joe Collins four times each.)

93. A slugger who once went hitless in a World Series drove home both runs in Johnny Podres's 2–0 victory over the Yankees in the seventh game of the 1955 Fall Classic. (He hit .370 career homers.) Who was he?

94. Whose three-run game-winning home run in game three turned the 1956 World Series around for the Yankees? (He played for the winning Cardinals against New York in 1942.)

95. One Yankees Cy Young Award winner won two of the last three games—and saved the other one—in the 1958 World Series. Who is he?

96. Who, besides Babe Ruth, hit the most World Series home runs by a left-handed batter? (He hit the first pinch-hit home run in Fall Classic play.)

97. Which National League player hit the most World Series home runs (11)? (A Hall of Famer, he was a .295 lifetime hitter.)

98. Name the pitcher who in the final game of the 1968 World Series picked off two Cardinals base runners in the same inning en route to a 4–1 win. (He outpitched Bob Gibson, ending the Redbirds pitcher's record seven-game winning streak.)

99. The two opposing catchers in the 1976 World Series both hit well over .500. Who hit .533 and two homers for the winners?

100. Who hit .529 for the losers? (From 1976 to 1978, he caught in three consecutive World Series, starring twice for the winners.)

Chapter Nine Answers

1. Orel Hershiser
2. Wes Parker
3. Stan Musial (1950–52 Cardinals)
4. Gaylord Perry
5. Goose Gossage
6. Orlando Cepeda
7. Willie McCovey
8. Dickie Kerr
9. Jim Palmer
10. Jim Rice (1977–78 and 1983)
11. Jackie Robinson
12. Al Rosen
13. Jim Bagby Sr. (31 in 1920; Jim Jr.)
14. Jim Hegan (Bob Feller, Bob Lemon, Gene Bearden, Mike Garcia, Early Wynn, and Herb Score)
15. Norm Cash (1961)
16. Spud Chandler (1943)
17. Eddie Collins (1910 and 1913 Philadelphia Athletics; 1917 White Sox)
18. LaMarr Hoyt (1983–84)
19. Schoolboy Row
20. John Wathan (Royals)

21. Joe Black (1952 Brooklyn Dodgers)
22. Jim "Mudcat" Grant (1965 Twins)
23. Bob Gibson (1967 Cardinals)
24. Reggie Jackson (Oakland A's)
25. Dave Kingman
26. Chuck Tanner (to Pittsburgh for Manny Sanguillen)
27. Dennis Eckersley (1989–90 Oakland A's)
28. Darold Knowles
29. Mickey Rivers
30. Roy Campanella (1951, 1953, and 1955 Brooklyn Dodgers)
31. Don Newcombe (1956 Brooklyn Dodgers)
32. Frank Robinson (1966 Orioles)
33. Elston Howard (1963 Yankees)
34. Jackie Robinson (1949 Brooklyn Dodgers)
35. J. R. Richard (1978–79 Astros)
36. Vida Blue (Oakland A's)
37. Bob Gibson (1964, 1967–68 Cardinals)
38. Mark Fidrych (1976)
39. Willie McCovey (1950s to 1980s)
40. Tommy Davis (1962–63 Los Angeles Dodgers)
41. Larry Doby (1948; 1952 and 1954 Indians)
42. Frank Robinson (1961 Reds and 1966 Orioles)
43. Ernie Banks (1958–59 Cubs)
44. Ben Oglivie
45. Gorman Thomas
46. Sam Jones (1955 Cubs)
47. Frank Robinson (1975 Indians and 1981 San Francisco Giants)
48. Willie Stargell (1971, 1973 Pirates)
49. Willie Mays

50. Dizzy Dean (Cardinals)
51. Arky Vaughan (1941 Pirates)
52. Rip Sewell (Pirates)
53. Ferguson Jenkins
54. Steve Garvey (Los Angeles Dodgers)
55. Mickey Rivers (Yankees)
56. Mike Cuellar (1970 Orioles)
57. Dave McNally (1970 Orioles)
58. Bert Blyleven
59. Jerry Reuss (Pirates and Los Angeles Dodgers)
60. Hank Bauer (1956 to 1958 Yankees)
61. Yogi Berra (Yankees)
62. Pee Wee Reese (1941, 1947, 1949, 1952–53, and 1956 Brooklyn Dodgers)
63. Fred Merkle (1911–13 New York Giants, 1916 Brooklyn Dodgers, and 1918 Cubs)
64. Pepper Martin (Cardinals; Mickey Cochrane)
65. Phil Rizzuto (1956; 1950)
66. Lou Gehrig (1928 and 1932 Yankees)
67. Willie Wilson (1980 and 1982 Royals)
68. Whitey Ford (Yankees)
69. Yogi Berra (1956)
70. Chris Sabo
71. Christy Mathewson (1905 New York Giants)
72. Dale Mitchell (1956 Brooklyn Dodgers)
73. Babe Pinelli
74. Jim Lonborg
75. Jim Palmer (Orioles)
76. Babe Ruth (1916 Red Sox)
77. Sherry Smith (1916 Brooklyn Dodgers)
78. Harry Brecheen (1943–44 and 1946)
79. Dickie Kerr

80. Waite Hoyt
81. Bill Klem
82. Earl McNeely
83. Mel Ott
84. Carl Hubbell (New York Giants)
85. Carl Hubbell (1936–37 New York Giants)
86. Hal Schumacher
87. Monte Pearson
88. Whit Wyatt
89. Hank Borowy (1945)
90. Hank Bauer
91. Johnny Mize (1939–40 Cardinals and 1947–48 Giants)
92. Carl Erskine
93. Gil Hodges (Brooklyn Dodgers)
94. Enos Slaughter
95. Bob Turley
96. Yogi Berra (12 with the Yankees; 1947)
97. Duke Snider (Brooklyn and Los Angeles Dodgers)
98. Mickey Lolich (Tigers)
99. Johnny Bench (Reds)
100. Thurman Munson (Yankees)

BONUS QUESTION #25
Before and After

Joe DiMaggio, of course, holds the record for hitting in the most consecutive games—56—in major-league history.

He broke the previous record of George Sisler of the Browns, who had hit safely in 41 consecutive games. Since DiMaggio broke Sisler's mark, the closest that any player in the American League has come to the "Clipper's" streak is 39.

Name the player who once got a record five hits in one World Series game.

BONUS QUESTION #26
The Eck-man

Dennis Eckersley is coming to the close of a celebrated career.

In 1992 he became one of only five relief pitchers to win both MVP and the Cy Young Award in the same season. That was the year in which he saved an incredible 51 games in 54 attempts. In 1990 he posted 48 saves and logged an all-time-low 0.61 ERA. In addition, he owns the American League saves record with 323, going into the 1996 season.

He was a starter when he broke into the majors in 1975. He has pitched a no-hitter, won 20 games in a season, and battled alcohol addiction.

We've got two questions on the Eck-man. With whom did he pitch his no-hitter? With whom did he win 20 games?

Chapter Nine Score

Number of Hits (Correct Answers)   _____

Number of At Bats (Questions)   _____

Season Batting Average   _____

Chapter Ten

Rickey, Mookie, and the Crow

1. Name the player who led his league in stolen bases a record 11 times. (He set the single-season record, too.)
2. Who was the only pitcher to win the Cy Young Award while hurling for a last-place club? (He struck out a league-leading 310 batters that year.)
3. Pinpoint the 300-game winner whose highest ERA over the last 15 years of his career was 2.60. (He was called "Gettysburg Eddie.")
4. What post–World War II Yankees pitcher won his only two World Series decisions in his rookie year? (He was the winning pitcher in the All-Star Game that year, too.)
5. Which pitcher from the 1940s won 21 games in his rookie year, 25 in his sophomore season, but

only 19 thereafter? (He was 1–0 with a 2.03 ERA in his only World Series, in 1946.)

6. Who was the slugger of the 1970s who hit 38 home runs in each of three consecutive years? (His all-time high was 48 in 1980.)

7. From 1924 to 1929 this .310 lifetime batter—who had seasons of most hits, doubles, triples, home runs and RBIs—averaged 126 runs batted in a year. Name him.

8. For which team did Archibald "Moonlight" Graham of *Field of Dreams* fame appear in his only major-league game? (It was in 1905.)

9. Winner of two games in the 1948 World Series and loser of two games in the 1954 Fall Classic, he started out as a third baseman and ended up winning 207 major-league games. Who is he?

10. Name the American League infielder—a .314 career batter—who hit .300 eight times before serving in World War II, but never higher than .252 after returning from the service.

11. What Detroit pitcher, a winner of just three games during his major-league career, shut out Bob Feller on the last day of the 1940 season, allowing the Tigers to edge the Indians for the pennant?

12. Whose 50 consecutive stolen bases from 1988 to 1989 is a record? (He is the only player to steal 100 or more bases in his first three seasons.)

13. What pitcher had 20-win seasons for the 1969 Los Angeles Dodgers and the 1973 Angels? (He pitched a no-hitter for the 1970 Dodgers.)

14. Who was the Brooklyn outfielder that Richie Ashburn threw out at the plate in the bottom of

the ninth inning of the last game of the 1950
season to prevent the Dodgers from winning the
flag? (The Phillies won the game and the pennant in the next inning on Dick Sisler's three-
run homer.)

15. Reach back in time to identify the first baseman
whom the Pirates fired after he struck out 10
times in the 1909 World Series. (Pittsburgh defeated the Tigers in seven games.)

16. Identify the New York Mets and Yankees manager who grounded into a record-tying four double plays in one game. (He won the 1971 batting
title and MVP award with the Cardinals.)

17. What American League first baseman became
the only player to twice hit two home runs in a
single game in the same Series? (He hit his first
major-league triple in the 1980 World Series.)

18. Who was the Tigers and Red Sox batting champ
whose promising career came to a close the following year when he was seriously burned during a diathermy treatment for an injured leg?
(He was a .331 lifetime hitter.)

19. Name the Phillies slugger and Rookie of the
Year who won his only two home run champi-
onships in the American League. (He won the
MVP award with the 1972 White Sox.)

20. Name the infielder who hit a record 123 career
sacrifice flies. (In the 1982 World Series he twice
got four hits, a record for one Classic.)

21. Name the former Met who got married at home
plate. (He stole a Met-record 58 bases in 1982.)

22. Which Met hit three home runs in four games

and batted .357 in the five-game triumph of the "Amazin' Ones" over the Orioles in the 1969 World Series? (He hit 28 home runs for the 1966 Pirates.)

23. Name the Browns third baseman who in back-to-back years (1937–38) smashed 29 and 34 home runs and drove home 118 runs in each season. (He ended his career with the 1945 Senators.)

24. Who was the 1978 Indian who hit for the cycle, getting each hit off a different pitcher? (Three times he hit better than 30 home runs in a season for Cleveland.)

25. Name the White Sox player who one year hit just six home runs but drove home 128 runs. (He hit a club-high .388 that year.)

26. Who was the Cardinals outfielder who, first, lost Tim Northrup's fly ball in the sun and, second, slipped as the ball sailed by him for the game-winning triple in game seven of the 1968 World Series?

27. Which American League batting title winner was traded after the season for the league's home run champ? (He batted .303 lifetime.)

28. Name the second baseman, playing in at least 150 games, who led his league in fewest strike-outs for a record 11 consecutive years. (He won the MVP award with the 1959 White Sox.)

29. Identify the Yankees second baseman who bowed out of the majors with a .364 batting average in the 1957 World Series. (He played on Fall Classic winners his first three years in the majors.)

30. What player averaged 109 stolen bases over the first three years of his career, a period during which he batted just .263? (He stole six bases in the 1987 World Series.)

31. Who drew a career-record 293 intentional bases on balls? (He also grounded into a career-record 328 double plays.)

32. Name the .294 lifetime hitter—a Hall of Fame third baseman—who player-managed his team to their first world title. (He won out over Fred Clarke of the Pirates.)

33. Identify the first switch-hitter to win a home run title. (He played for the "Gas House Gang.")

34. Who was the Yankee center fielder who once led his league with 231 hits and 23 triples? (He batted .350 in four World Series.)

35. Name the 1996 manager who won Rookie of the Year with the 1969 Royals. (He once managed a club to a World Series sweep.)

36. Who was the first baseman who teamed with Joe Gordon, Lou Boudreau, and Kenny Keltner to give the 1948 Indians an infield that averaged 108 RBIs. (He drove home 100 RBIs in each season from 1951 to 1953.)

37. Identify the Cardinals catcher who picked Joe Gordon off second base for the final out of the 1942 World Series. (In 1947, he hit 35 home runs and drove home 122 runs for the New York Giants.)

38. Who was the youngest recipient of the World Series MVP Award? (He won Cy Young awards in 1985 and 1989.)

39. Name the 1994 Cubs outfielder who hit a National League–record three home runs on opening day. (Dwight Gooden started for the Mets that day.)

40. Who was the only American League player to pinch-hit home runs in both ends of a doubleheader? (A onetime player manager, he is now in the Hall of Fame.)

41. Though he batted just .245 lifetime and .174 in seven World Series, this infielder's teams won six world titles when he played in each one of its games. (He later coached in many World Series with the Yankees.)

42. In the last season of his 15-year career, he lost the batting title by one point to the Yankees' George Stirnweiss, but he never played in another game. Who was this long-time coach for manager Al Lopez?

43. Name the Red Sox substitute center fielder for the injured Dom DiMaggio whom the Cardinals' Enos Slaughter tested when he scored the winning run of the 1946 World Series, all the way from first base, on a "double" by Harry Walker.

44. Identify the 1947 Tigers first baseman who finished fourth in the home run race and second in the bases-on-balls department, yet never played in another major-league game. (Three years apart, 1942 and 1945, he played in World Series with the Yankees and the Tigers.)

45. Who was the .291 lifetime hitter who drilled a record three home runs for the 1954 Cardinals,

in his first two games in the majors? (Nevertheless, he hit only 64 circuit clouts in 12 seasons.)

46. Benched in the 1927 World Series by Pittsburgh manager Donie Bush because he objected to a change of positions in the batting order, this .321 lifetime batter watched impassively as the 1927 "Murderers' Row" Yankees swept the Pirates in four games. (After the season he was traded to the Cubs.) Who was this Hall of Famer?

47. He played in more games, registered more at-bats, scored more runs, collected more hits, slashed more doubles, slammed more triples, ran more total bases, and batted in more runs than any other Senators player. Who was he?

48. Identify the shortstop who twice, in two tries, hit .400 for the New York Giants in the World Series. (He once managed them into the seventh game of a World Series.)

49. Can you name the only Brooklyn Dodgers player to win back-to-back batting titles? (This lifetime .303 batter played all 2,001 of his career games at first base.)

50. Name the Twins player who led the American League in triples in three straight seasons. (In 1965 he won the MVP Award.)

51. Who was the first slugger to win four consecutive home run titles? (He played in three World Series for the Philadelphia Athletics.)

52. In Sandy Koufax's last game, a 6–0 loss to the Orioles' Jim Palmer in the second game of the 1966 World Series, he was victimized by this

outfielder, who made three errors in one inning. (The culprit stole 398 career bases.)

53. A .308 hitter over 16 years, this National League catcher 10 times batted .300 and, six times in six full years with the Phillies, topped the .300 mark. (He also caught for the Cardinals, Reds, and Pirates.) Who was he?

54. Lou Gehrig hit a record 23 grand slams with the 1923–39 Yankees. Who leads the National League with 18 four-run round-trippers? (He hit the most career home runs by a left-handed batter in National League history.)

55. Who was the 1982–86 Angels third baseman who averaged 23 home runs per season? (He succeeded an all-time great from another team at his position.)

56. A .345 lifetime hitter, this player twice hit .400 for the Phillies in the 1890s. (Once he hit .399; another time, he batted .397. In 1902 he won a batting title with the Senators.) Who was this early baseball star who seven times drove home more than 100 runs in a season.

57. He won four batting titles and hit almost 800 home runs in the Negro Leagues. Twice he hit more than 70 home runs in a season. Name this star who died in the year Jackie Robinson was admitted to the major leagues.

58. Which one of the following Yankee catchers did not twice hit .400 in World Series play: Bill Dickey, Yogi Berra, Elston Howard, or Thurman Munson?

59. What pitcher was the only Twins hurler to lose

20 games in a season? (He once led the American League in losses for a record four consecutive years.)

60. Who was the Yankee who in three consecutive World Series batted safely in 15 of 16 games? (In the 1976–77 World Series he had seven consecutive hits.)

61. Identify the Browns third baseman who led the American League in stolen bases from 1947 to 1949. (He was a .306 lifetime hitter.)

62. Name the player whose 34-game batting streak was broken when his outfielder brother raced down his final bid to keep the mark alive. (He led the American League in stolen bases with the 1950 Red Sox.)

63. Who was the Senators strongman who hit a record 10 home runs in one week? (He won home run crowns in 1968 and 1970.)

64. Name the home run–hitting outfielder of the 1930s and 1940s in the National League who led his loop in strikeouts in six of his 10 seasons. (He was perhaps the best-fielding center fielder of three big-name brothers.)

65. What player hit three home runs in a game a record six times but didn't play on the winning team in any of those contests? (He hit 359 major-league home runs.)

66. What Red Sox second baseman averaged 106 RBIs a season over the last six years of his career? (He retired prematurely because of a bad back.)

67. A two-time 20-game winner, he won 25 games

for the 1901 Brooklyn Dodgers and 25 games for the 1907 Tigers. (He was one of the few pitchers to post 25 wins in each league.) Identify this pitcher, who was a member of the losing team in each of the 1907–9 World Series.

68. Name the pitcher who won just four more games after copping 25 contests during his Cy Young Award season. (Two years later, he was out of baseball.)

69. Though he was a .291 lifetime hitter, this Cardinals center fielder is best remembered as a defensive specialist. Who was this 1927 fly-hawk who registered a season's-record 547 putouts?

70. Identify the only opposing everyday player whom Bob Feller didn't strike out during the 1946 season, when he recorded 348 strikeouts. (The hitter had a .312 lifetime average.)

71. Who was the first of two players to hit two home runs in his first major-league game? (Bert Campaneris of the 1964 Kansas City Athletics was the other.) He was the only player to do it in his first two at bats.

72. "Laughing Larry" won the batting title in 1915, but he wasn't happy when the New York Giants traded him to the Cubs the following year. Who was this second baseman?

73. What Yankee first baseman after Lou Gehrig won a home run title? (He won the crown with 22 four-base blows.) Who was he?

74. Who played on world title teams his first four years and Fall Classic championship clubs his

last three seasons? (He played in 10 World Series, nine times on the winning team.)

75. Name the pitcher who hurled a record three consecutive shutouts in one World Series. (He also pitched a record ten complete games in Fall Classic play.)

76. In 22 years of playing, he batted .280 and performed on three consecutive pennant winners; in 21 years of managing, his teams never finished higher than third, though. (He certainly wasn't a "push-button" manager, a tag he placed on Joe McCarthy of the Yankees.) Name him.

77. From 1950 to 1952 he slugged 86 home runs. Who was this 240-pound, left-handed power hitter for the Indians?

78. The 1948 Boston Braves were powered to the National League pennant by a third baseman who hit 23 home runs and drove home 100 runs. (The year before, he won the MVP award.) Who was he?

79. The post–World War II Phillies had an outfielder who recorded a .284 lifetime average and slugged 288 career homers. Who was that slugger whom the Philadelphia fans loved to boo?

80. In three World Series at bats he hit two homers. Who was that 1959 Los Angeles Dodger?

81. A wartime standout, he led the American League in home runs in 1944 and RBIs in 1945. Who was that Yankee first baseman?

82. Name the player who hit a single-season-record 11 home runs as a leadoff batter? (He had 30-

home-run seasons with the San Francisco Giants, the Yankees, the Angels, and the White Sox-Rangers.)

83. Outfielders Vic Wertz, Hoot Evers, and what center fielder all hit .300 for the 1950 Tigers? (It was his only .300 season over a 15-year career.)

84. Who was the Red Sox player who in the strike-abbreviated season of 1981 ended up in the only four-way tie for a home run title? (He hit .300 and clubbed a total of three home runs in the 1975 and 1986 World Series.)

85. Who was the last Philadelphia Athletics player to win a batting title? (He copped it in back-to-back years.)

86. Name the Hall of Famer who played for the Cubs and the White Sox and managed the Bruins and the Pale Hose. (He was nicknamed both the Trojan and the Crab.)

87. Name the only left-handed pitcher to record 300 career saves? (He was pitching in 1996.)

88. Identify the speedster from the Dominican Republic who stole 550 bases over a 17-year career, climaxing it between 1972 and 1977, a period in which he stole 50 or more bases every season.

89. Name the American League player, in addition to Ty Cobb, who won six batting titles in a seven-year period. (He did it in the 1970s.)

90. Once a teenage star with the Cubs, he went on to bat .462 in the 1938 World Series and .423 in the 1945 Fall Classic, both times with the Bruins. Who is he?

91. What 1958 Los Angeles Dodgers rookie went on

to play 1,000 games at both first base and the outfield? (He played in four World Series with the Dodgers, batting .300.)

92. Who was the White Sox–Indian outfielder who batted over .300 in eight of his nine years? (A .314 lifetime batter, he was called "Jockey.")

93. This Hall of Fame receiver batted .281 over an 18-year career and caught his brother, who hit .280 over a 15-year span. Who is he?

94. Who picked up a record six saves in the World Series? (He chalked them up in three consecutive fall classics.)

95. Who was the only catcher to hit more than 300 home runs and steal more than 100 bases in his career? (He was an American Leaguer.)

96. In 1900, with the Phillies, he batted .378 but lost the batting title by three points to Honus Wagner; in 1906, with the Indians, he hit .306 but edged out Willie Keeler by four points for the hitting crown. Who was this Hall of Famer, who batted .315 lifetime?

97. Name the Cardinals outfielder of the 1960s who batted .306 over an eight-year span (1961–68), during which time he posted back-to-back (1963–64) 200-hit seasons?

98. Who was the last Indians player to "win" the batting title? (It was later taken away from him on a technicality and given to Ted Williams.)

99. A lesser-known name than Napoleon Lajoie, Elmer Flick, and Tris Speaker, with the Indians, this member of the Tribe also won a batting title.

But with a .369 mark in 1929 and a .316 lifetime average, you should know him. Who was he?

100. A .270 hitter with 121 home runs over 11 years, he hit the first home run at the new Yankee Stadium. Who was this 1976 Twins outfielder?

The Wrap-up Question

1001. Who hit the most home runs (9) in a career without hitting one of them over the fence? (He managed an American League team to three world championships.)

Chapter Ten Answers

1. Rickey Henderson (1980–86 and 1988–91 Oakland A's and Yankees)
2. Steve Carlton (1972 Phillies)
3. Eddie Plank (1903–17 Philadelphia Athletics, St. Louis, Federal team, and St. Louis Browns)
4. Frank "Spec" Shea (1947)
5. Dave "Boo" Ferriss (1945–48 Red Sox)
6. Mike Schmidt (Phillies)
7. Jim Bottomley (Cardinals)
8. Giants
9. Bob Lemon (Indians)
10. Cecil Travis (1933–47 Senators)
11. Floyd Giebell
12. Vince Coleman (1985–87 Cardinals)
13. Bill Singer
14. Cal Abrams
15. Bill Abstein
16. Joe Torre (1975 Mets)

17. Willie Aikens (1980 Royals)
18. David Dale Alexander
19. Richie Allen (1972 and 1974 White Sox)
20. Robin Yount (1974–93 Brewers)
21. Mookie Wilson (1978, Jackson, Mississippi)
22. Donn Clendenon
23. Harlond Clift
24. Andre Thornton (1978, 1982, and 1984)
25. Luke Appling (1936)
26. Curt Flood
27. Harvey Kuenn of Detroit was traded to Cleveland for Rocky Colavito.
28. Nellie Fox (1952–62 White Sox)
29. Gerry Coleman (1949–51)
30. Vince Coleman (1985–87 Cardinals)
31. Hank Aaron
32. Jimmy Collins (1903 Red Sox)
33. James "Ripper" Collins (1934 Cardinals)
34. Earle Combs (1927)
35. Lou Piniella (1990 Reds)
36. Eddie Robinson (White Sox and Athletics)
37. Walker Cooper
38. Bret Saberhagen (21 in 1985; 1985 and 1989 Royals)
39. Karl Rhodes
40. Joe Cronin of the 1943 Red Sox sent himself up to pinch-hit both times.
41. Frank Crosetti (Yankees, who later became a coach)
42. Tony Cuccinello (1945 White Sox)
43. Leon Culberson

44. Roy Cullenbine
45. Joe Cunningham
46. Kiki Cuyler
47. Sam Rice
48. Al Dark (1951, 1954 New York Giants, and 1962 San Francisco Giants)
49. Jake Daubert (1913–14)
50. Zoilo Versalles (1963–65)
51. Harry Davis (1904–7)
52. Willie Davis
53. Virgil "Spud" Davis (1929–33 and 1939)
54. Willie McCovey (521)
55. Doug DeCinces (Brooks Robinson of the Orioles)
56. Ed Delahanty
57. Josh Gibson (1947)
58. Thurman Munson
59. Pedro Ramos (1961; 1958–60 Senators and 1961 Twins)
60. Thurman Munson (1976–1978)
61. Bob Dillinger
62. Dom DiMaggio (Joe)
63. Frank Howard (1968 Senators)
64. Vince DiMaggio (Braves, Pirates, and Phillies)
65. Johnny Mize (Cardinals, New York Giants, and Yankees)
66. Bobby Doerr (1946–51)
67. Wild Bill Donovan
68. Steve Stone (1980–81 Orioles)
69. Taylor Douthit
70. Barney McCosky (Tigers and Athletics)

71. Bob Nieman (1951 Browns)
72. Larry Doyle
73. Nick Etten (1944)
74. Joe DiMaggio (1936–39 and 1949–51 Yankees)
75. Christy Mathewson (1905 New York Giants)
76. Jimmy Dykes
77. Luke Easter
78. Bob Elliott
79. Del Ennis
80. Chuck Essegian (he pinch-hit both home runs for the 1959 Los Angeles Dodgers)
81. Nick Etten
82. Bobby Bonds
83. Johnny Groth
84. Dwight Evans
85. Ferris Fain (1951–52)
86. Johnny Evers
87. John Franco (1984–96 Reds and Mets)
88. Cesar Cedeno (Astros)
89. Rod Carew (1972–75 and 1977–78 Twins)
90. Phil Cavarretta
91. Ron Fairly
92. Bibb Falk
93. Rick Ferrell
94. Rollie Fingers (1972–74 Oakland A's)
95. Carlton Fisk (Red Sox and White Sox, 375 and 128)
96. Elmer Flick
97. Curt Flood
98. Bobby Avila

99. Lew Fonseca
100. Dan Ford

The Wrap-up Question Answer

1001. Miller Huggins (1904–16 Reds and Cardinals;
1923, 1927–28 Yankees)

Chapter Ten Score

Number of Hits (Correct Answers)   _____

Number of At Bats (Questions)   _____

Season Batting Average   _____

Total Score

Number of Hits (Correct Answers)   _____
Number of At bats (Questions) 1,000   _____
Career Batting Average   _____

BONUS QUESTION #27
Steady Eddie

He's never won a batting crown. He's never won a home run crown outright.

But he's collected more than 3,000 hits, and he's hit more career home runs than any other player who has never won a four-base title outright.

Name this player who holds the record of 19 consecutive seasons of 75 or more runs batted in.

Your Career Batting Average

The following players are listed from the top to almost the bottom in career averages. See with whom you match up.

If your average surpasses Ty Cobb's all-time-high .367, you are in a league all your own. A mark between .325 and .366 places you with baseball's elite. You are just about guaranteed to be a Hall of Famer if your average lies between .300 and .324.

You are a good player if your batting average falls between .275 and .299. A mark between .250 and .274 places you in the average category. One between .225 and .249 indicates that you are a sub-average hitter. Finally, an average between .200 and .224 sends up a distress signal that you are approaching the "Mendoza Line."

But take heart! Back when there were 16 traditional teams, there were only 400 players in the major leagues. Today, with 28 clubs, there are 700 players in the big leagues.

If you batted .200 or over, you made it. You're a big leaguer. Congratulations!

.367 Ty Cobb
.359 Rogers Hornsby
.356 Joe Jackson
.349 Lefty O'Doul
.346 Ed Delahanty
.345 Tris Speaker
.344 Ted Williams
.342 Babe Ruth
.341 Bill Terry
.340 Lou Gehrig
.339 Nap Lajoie
.336 Riggs Stephenson
.334 Al Simmons
.333 Paul Waner
.331 Stan Musial
.330 Heinie Manush
.328 Rod Carew
.327 Honus Wagner
.325 Joe DiMaggio
.324 Joe Medwick
.322 Sam Rice
.321 Kiki Cuyler
.320 Mickey Cochrane
.319 Ken Williams
.318 Arky Vaughan
.317 Roberto Clemente
.316 Frankie Frisch
.315 Fred Clarke
.314 Cecil Travis
.313 Bill Dickey
.312 Johnny Mize
.311 Jackie Robinson

.310 Luke Appling
.309 Sam Crawford
.308 Richie Ashburn
.307 Frank "Home Run" Baker
.306 Dixie Walker
.305 Hank Aaron
.304 Tony Oliva
.303 Pete Rose
.302 Willie Mays
.301 Joe Cronin
.300 Pedro Guerrero
.299 Carl Furillo
.298 Mickey Mantle
.297 Al Kaline
.296 Ken Griffey Sr.
.295 Mickey Rivers
.294 Frank Robinson
.293 Monte Irvin
.292 Thurman Munson
.291 Lou Piniella
.290 Hal McRae
.289 Bob Elliott
.288 Bobby Doerr
.287 Reggie Smith
.286 Vada Pinson
.285 Al Rosen
.284 Wally Schang
.283 Dave Cash
.282 Ken Singleton
.281 Danny Litwhiler
.280 Jesus Alou
.279 Willie Davis

.278 Cesar Tovar
.277 Hank Bauer
.276 Danny Cater
.275 Jimmy Sheckard
.274 Elston Howard
.273 Gil Hodges
.272 Norm Siebern
.271 Don Kolloway
.270 Willie McCovey
.269 Red Ruffing
.268 Bill Nicholson
.267 Mike Schmidt
.266 Bobby Grich
.265 Ollie Brown
.264 Dick Stuart
.263 Bill Russell
.262 Reggie Jackson
.261 Ron Cey
.260 Don Baylor
.259 Bill Rigney
.258 Mike Cubbage
.257 Billy Martin
.256 Harmon Killebrew
.255 Tommie Agee
.254 Max West
.253 Ray Schalk
.252 Davey Williams
.251 Rico Petrocelli
.250 Paul Blair
.249 Everett Scott
.248 Graig Nettles
.247 Tommy Thevenow

.246 Chris Speier
.245 Frank Crosetti
.244 Sal Yvars
.243 Andy Seminick
.242 Cliff Mapes
.241 Gene Tenace
.240 Bobby Bragan
.239 Gene Mauch
.238 Eddie Miller
.237 Billy Gardner
.236 Eddie O'Brien
.235 Don Zimmer
.234 Ruben Amaro
.233 Clay Dalrymple
.232 Buck Rodgers
.231 Bob Swift
.230 Frank Dwyer
.229 Bobby Del Greco
.228 Steve Yeager
.227 Rube Walker
.226 Zinn Beck
.225 Buck Martinez
.224 Ed Brinkman
.223 Sam Bowens
.222 Johnnie LeMaster
.221 Billy Consolo
.220 Chuck Cottier
.219 Skeeter Webb
.218 Alex Gaston
.217 Dal Maxvill
.216 Pat Corrales
.215 Mario Mendoza

.214 Dave Duncan
.213 Dick Tracewski
.212 Ned Yost
.211 Jack Heidemann
.210 Luis Gomez
.209 Al Glossop
.208 Sam Crane
.207 Sammy Esposito
.206 Leo Dixon
.205 Buddy Biancalana
.204 Carl Nichols
.203 Hal Finney
.202 Merrill Combs
.201 Cliff Cook
.200 Bob Uecker

Bonus Question Answers

Introduction. Ed Head of the Dodgers, Larry Jansen of the New York Giants, and Bill Bevens of the Yankees

1. *Super Sleuths.* Maury Wills (Los Angeles Dodgers)
2. *Batting Ch(u)mps.* Heinie Zimmerman (Triple Crown in 1912) and Hal Chase
3. *Surprise Starter.* Howard Ehmke
4. *The Streakers.* Everett Scott
5. *The Deacon.* Bill McKechnie
6. *Beating the Depression.* Lefty O'Doul
7. *Twinkletoes.* George Selkirk
8. *Rapid Rise.* Bob Feller
9. *Hammerin' Hank.* Bob Feller
10. *The Dutch Master.* Leo Durocher
11. *Twenty-Twenty.* Bobo Newsom
12. *Baseball's Best Wartime Team.* Ted Wilks
13. *The Brat.* Eddie Stanky (1947 Brooklyn Dodgers, 1948 Boston Braves, and 1951 New York Giants)
14. *Tiny.* Ernie Bonham
15. *A Close Shave.* Sal "the Barber" Maglie
16. *Déjà Vu.* Herb Score
17. *A Long Out.* Vic Wertz
18. *Making Their Hits Count.* Pete Runnels

19. *The Monster.* Dick Radatz
20. *Speaking of Shortstops.* Luis Aparicio
21. *The Year of the Pitcher.* Orel Hershiser (Los Angeles Dodgers)
22. *The Reserve Clause.* Curt Flood
23. *The Secretary of Defense.* Garry Maddox
24. *They Could Hit.* Rod Carew (1977 Twins and 1983 Angels)
25. *Before and After.* Paul Molitor (1987 Brewers; 1982 Brewers)
26. *The Eck-man.* (1977 Indians and 1978 Red Sox)
27. *Steady Eddie.* Eddie Murray

Your Career World Series Batting Average

The following players are listed from the top to the bottom in career World Series batting averages. See with whom you match up.

If your average surpasses Billy Hatcher's all-time high .750, you are in a league all your own. Hatcher had 9 hits in 12 at bats in the 1990 Fall Classic. A mark between .400 and .500 places you with some of the greatest clutch hitters in the history of the game.

You are a good World Series player if your batting average falls between .295 and .399. A mark between .256 and .294 indicates that you are a good regular-season player, but you played below par in the Fall Classic. One between .200 and .255 signifies that you are a sub-average hitter. Finally, an average below .200 sends you a signal that you might be "riding the pines" in your next World Series.

Perhaps you just ran into some hot pitchers while you were swinging a cold bat.

But once again, take comfort. George Sisler, Luke Appling, Ernie Banks, and Don Mattingly never played in a World Series. You did.

Keep swinging!

World Series (Bonus Questions) Score

Number of Hits (Correct Answers)   _____

Number of At bats (Questions) 30   _____

Career World Series Average   _____

.750 Billy Hatcher
.500 Vic Wertz
.439 Bobby Brown
.418 Pepper Martin
.400 Hal McRae
.391 Lou Brock
.373 George Brett
.364 Hank Aaron
.363 Frank Baker
.362 Roberto Clemente
.361 Lou Gehrig
.357 Reggie Jackson
.352 Carl Yastrzemski
.350 Earle Combs
.348 Stan Hack

.345 Joe Jackson
.344 Jimmie Foxx
.333 Billy Martin
.333 Julian Javier
.321 Charlie Gehringer
.319 Steve Garvey
.311 Tim McCarver
.308 Bill Mazeroski
.300 Spike Owen
.295 Mel Ott
.286 Johnny Mize
.271 Joe DiMaggio
.267 Gil Hodges
.257 Mickey Mantle
.256 Stan Musial
.246 Cesar Geronimo
.239 Willie Mays
.225 Bob Meusel
.214 Bill Nicholson
.208 Darryl Strawberry
.200 Ted Williams
.192 Tony Oliva
.185 Tommy Holmes
.170 Frank White
.167 Cal Ripken
.156 Jose Canseco
.149 Travis Jackson
.136 Dave Winfield
.125 Sixto Lezcano
.111 Bill White
.100 Al Zarilla
.095 Kenny Keltner

.080 Billy North
.061 Marv Owen
.053 Dick Sisler
.000 Birdie Tebbetts